Lorna Chaplin first visited the Cyclades island of Paros in 1979 on a two-week package holiday and fell in love with it at once. Return visits were limited while she completed her nursing training but Paros has been her home since February 1984 where she lives in the middle of nowhere with her two cats.

To Neddy (Edna) Chaplin for
so many reasons, the very least
of which being that she typed
the manuscript.

About this book

Having extensively used travel guides within Greece and South East
Asia, I have tried to include in this book the things I have often
wished were in those on which I have previously depended.

I have substituted historical data and descriptions of church
interiors with explanations of how to find hotels, post offices etc.
in the belief that those visitors with a keen interest in archaeology
or old churches will probably buy one of the specialist books on
these subjects.

It is meant as no insult to the readers' intelligence that I have,
where possible, recommended eating places. Of course part of the
fun of a holiday is to wander at leisure around the towns and
villages and find a favourite taverna; but on your first day perhaps
a little travel weary, you may be grateful for some suggestions.

If you speak the language then finding things presents no
problem, but Greek as a second language is rare; hence the
directions under useful addresses.

The language chapter is meant to help only in emergencies and
is no substitute for a phrase book. Apart from place names, all
Greek words have been spelt phonetically. The accent denotes the
syllable to be stressed.

Prices, hotel names and standards can change almost overnight.
Last year's supermarket can be this year's boutique, *taverna* or
disco. Successive editions will endeavour to keep all information
as up-to-date and accurate as possible.

Have a great time!

Acknowledgements

The author would like to thank Panayotis Boudouris and his
charming wife Dina for their considerable help in the researching
of this book.

Greek Island Series

North West Cyclades

Lorna Chaplin

Andros · Kea · Kythnos · Serifos
Syros and Tinos

Roger Lascelles, Cartographic and Travel Publisher
47 York Road, Brentford, Middlesex TW8 0QP Telephone: 01-847 0935

Publication Data

Title	North West Cyclades
Typeface	Phototypeset in Compugraphic Times
Photographs	Lorna Chaplin
Printing	Kelso Graphics, Kelso, Scotland.
ISBN	0 903909 56 1
Edition	This first February, 1987
Publisher	Roger Lascelles
	47 York Road, Brentford, Middlesex, TW8 0QP.
Copyright	Lorna Chaplin

Distribution

Africa:	South Africa —	Faradawn, Box 17161, Hillbrow 2038
Americas:	Canada —	International Travel Maps & Books, P.O. Box 2290, Vancouver BC V6B 3W5.
	U.S.A. —	Hunter Publishing Inc, 155 Riverside Dr, New York NY 10024 (212) 595 8933
Asia:	Hong Kong —	The Book Society, G.P.O. Box 7804, Hong Kong 5-241901
	India —	English Book Store, 17-L Connaught Circus/P.O. Box 328, New Delhi 110 001
	Singapore —	Graham Brash Pte Ltd., 36-C Prinsep St.
Australasia	Australia —	Rex Publications, 413 Pacific Highway, Artarmon NSW 2064. 428 3566
	New Zealand —	Enquiries invited.
Europe:	Belgium —	Brussels - Peuples et Continents
	Germany —	Available through major booksellers with good foreign travel sections
	GB/Irleand —	Available through all booksellers with good foreign travel sections.
	Italy —	Libreria dell'Automobile, Milano
	Netherlands —	Nilsson & Lamm BV, Weesp
	Denmark —	Copenhagen - Arnold Busck, G.E.C. Gad, Boghallen, G.E.C. Gad
	Finland —	Helsinki — Akateeminen Kirjakauppa
	Norway —	Oslo - Arne Gimnes/J.G. Tanum
	Sweden —	Stockholm/Esselte, Akademi Bokhandel, Fritzes, Hedengrens. Gothenburg/Gumperts, Esselte Lund/Gleerupska
	Switzerland —	Basel/Bider: Berne/Atlas; Geneve/Artou; Lausanne/Artou: Zurich/Travel Bookshop

Contents

Part 1: Planning Your Holiday

Part 2: The North West Cycladic Islands

ONE

Why a holiday in the Greek Islands?

No matter where you live in Britain, whether it be in a depressingly grim industrial area or a quaint rural village, the Greek islands are so different, so "un-British". There are islands where it is possible to imagine an advertising company having designed every feature in such a style as would make it most appealing to visitors. Tiny white sugar cubes have shutters and doors painted all the colours of the rainbow side by side with flaming geraniums and bougainvilia to make the brightest display. There's higgledy piggledy town planning with mazes of winding streets containing picture postcard courtyards and balconies; grey flagstones with the joins painstakingly whitewashed and here and there a magnificent forsythia or clematis springing from the tiniest cracks between them; harbours and shorelines dotted with little fishing boats lovingly painted in the most brilliant colours by their proud owners, who can be seen at sunset tenderising octopus on the rocks before hanging them up to dry.

The street displays of the shops rival that of any Eastern bazaar and the cries can be heard of the traders who peddle fruit, vegetables and fish from baskets attached to the saddles of enigmatic looking donkeys; road traffic consists of octogenarians riding donkeys and mules, overtaken by the ever-so-slightly faster drivers of rotovator engines attached to their two wheeled carts.

Fields of impossibly red poppies and sunkissed daisies inspire even those who have never before looked twice at a wild flower; here are rolling hills, rocky mountains with a house, chapel or monastery gouged seemingly inaccessibly into them; dry stone walls, ramshackle farm buildings, goitre-necked cattle, indignant turkeys, skittish sheep and vociferous farm dogs.

The pace of life and attitude to it are summarised by the custom of asking anyone seen looking at their watch if they are taking antibiotics. What other reason could you have for needing to know

9

Repairing the nets.

what time it is!

How fresh seems the enthusiasm on the faces of the dancers who are lured to the floor by the bazouki music, like sailors to the sirens; the generosity and hospitality of anyone whose threshhold you cross. How the conversations full of shouting and gesticulating contrast with the unearthly quiet of siesta time. Get the picture? It is just gloriously different!

Greece has facilities to suit all holiday requirements but if your criterion is to have everything the same as back home with sunshine to go with it, then probably the smaller islands would be wasted on you. Spanish resorts have adequate supplies of English fish and chips, English tea, English pubs (apologies to the Welsh and Scots) — and I for one hope it never happens to the Greek Islands.

The North West Cycladic Islands

The Cyclades Islands lie to the south east of the southern tip of mainland Greece and are so named because they are arranged in a rough circle. Of the twenty-eight islands in this group, two-thirds are inhabited. Of the north western islands covered by this book, only Giaros is uncolonised. Now used for military exercises, the island has a disused political prison from the days of the Junta.

Where a choice of spelling of island and town names exists, I have opted for that most closely resembling the form used on the island itself. In most cases, the main town has the same name as the island itself but the locals and bus timetables nearly always use the word Hora or Xora in place of the normal name. Many travel guides spell this word as Chora having explained somewhere in the volume that the Greek letter X is pronounced as the ch in the Scottish word loch. But having seen the locals struggle with my surname until it is turned into Kaplin or Tsaplin, I can't see the sense in this!

Andros A much maligned island in some guide books. I have found it one of the most beautiful both for its landscapes and buildings. The choice exists here between a small tourist town or many peaceful villages. A wealthy and mountainous verdant island with a good selection of beaches.

11

Kea A very uncommercialised, friendly but poor island, Kea offers the setting for getting away from it all. An anomaly exists between the lack of accommodation in the port and main town and the enormous hotel complex on the south west coast that is not served by public transport. It would probably be a more popular destination if connected more frequently to Piraeus rather than Lavrion, two hours by bus from Athens.

Kythnos A fairly new recipient of tourist visitors, this island is attempting to organise facilities for them, so at the moment it remains much as it was before this advent. Whilst not terribly picturesque, Kythnos has a certain primitive charm.

Serifos A pretty and quiet island with no more than a thousand inhabitants who mostly pursue a very rural, lonely existence. Apart from the unobtrusive tourist facilities in the port, the island is completely undeveloped.

Syros The commercial capital of the Cyclades, Syros is a terminus for island-hoppers as it has connections with so many islands. Worthy of visitors, the island is probably not as popular as it might be because the first sight on arrival is of the dry rocks and gas holding tanks — and these may well discourage those with a flexible itinerary from exploring the rest of the island which has some charming and attractive villages. All facilities exist here for both a lively and energetic or a relaxing family holiday.

Tinos For more than a hundred years, Tinos has been visited twice yearly by thousands upon thousands of pilgrims. The church at the top of the hill in the port is the Lourdes of the Aegean and so the island is far from typical. Tourism is now well established here and two of Britain's largest tour companies organise package holidays to a holiday centre just outside the main town. In addition to many dovecots, the island has numerous picturesque villages nestling in the valleys of the mountainous interior.

Official information

The National Tourist Office of Greece (N.T.O.G.) Known in Greece as E.O.T. (pronounced like yacht), this organisation is generally helpful and friendly. The British branch is at 195/197 Regent Street, London W1R 8DR. Nearest underground stations Oxford Circus and Piccadilly Circus.

The bulky pamphlet *General Information about Greece* is packed with facts, figures and relevant data that cover most queries. Specific to the Cyclades is a fourteen-page leaflet with many colour illustrations that gives hotel details and a brief summary of each island including all those covered in this book.

Offices on the Greek mainland relevant to this book are at:

— Piraeus: 105, Vassilissis Sofias Str.
— Athens: East Main Airport, Eliniko
— Athens: National Bank of Greece, 1 Karageorgi Servias Street. The latter is on a corner of Syntagma Square in Athens and has an enquiry desk where the multilingual staff are equipped with numerous handouts, maps and brochures which cover most enquiries. They produce a weekly summarised boat timetable of departures from Piraeus which can be invaluable.

Tourist police There used to be a separate tourist police force equipped with armbands bearing the flags of the countries whose language they spoke. Although signs marked 'Tourist Police Station' are still the thing to look for, these are mostly now within the regular police offices and an officer of the day will be allocated to deal with any complaints or queries and dispense information leaflets and maps to visitors. Some of them even speak a language other than Greek!

Visas

For those holding a British or Irish passport the entry stamp entitles you to stay for three months. Renewal is a complicated procedure that involves getting a form from a notary, completing it (it is printed in Greek only), buying stamps from another office, providing five passport photographs, evidence that you have changed money and have means of support for the next three months and generally satisfying the police that you are not working. The length of the extended stay is at the discretion of the police.

TWO

When to go

Between November and March the weather is very unpredictable, days of gales and torrential rain alternate with sunny blue skies and warm breezes so gentle that the sea is mirror-like.

The locals think it unwise to swim in the sea before Easter, at which time it will have been pleasantly hot for at least a month. Little old ladies in their multilayered black widow's weeds will touch your bare sun bronzed arm and enquire with a look of disbelief, "Surely you are cold!" Heaven help you if you get hayfever or sneeze in their presence, it sprouts "I told you so" looks!

From April to October the sun can be pretty much relied upon to make cooling off in the sea necessary, although it rarely gets uncomfortably hot in the shade.

In July and August the *Sirroco,* a warm but energetic wind from North Africa, can make trying to eat outside in the evening rather interesting! It usually lasts for three days at a time and alternates with a *meltemi,* a northerly wind that is generally cooler but less strong.

All meteorological details given are those issued by the station on the Cycladic Island of Naxos.

Average monthly atmospheric air temperatures in C°

	Jan	Feb	Mar	Apr	May	Jun
max	14.6	15.0	16.0	18.9	22.2	25.7
min	9.5	9.3	10.3	12.7	15.6	19.5
	Jul	Aug	Sept	Oct	Nov	Dec
max	27.0	27.1	24.9	22.3	19.6	16.3
min	21.8	22.0	19.8	17.0	14.0	11.4

Average temperatures of sea surface in C° at 14.00 hours					
Jan	Feb	Mar	Apr	May	Jun
15.0	14.9	15.1	16.8	19.1	22.2
Jul	Aug	Sep	Oct	Nov	Dec
23.9	23.5	22.7	20.0	17.4	15.5

Average number of days rain					
Jan	Feb	Mar	Apr	May	Jun
15.4	11.0	10.1	6.8	4.2	2.1
Jul	Aug	Sep	Oct	Nov	Dec
0.5	0.5	2.2	6.8	8.3	14.1

The sea temperature seems to vary from beach to beach and of course the hotter you get, the colder the sea feels!

All ferries, no matter how large, do not sail in winds of force 9 (and sometimes 8) on the Beaufort scale. These gales can spring up within hours and so beware! — plans including last minute sailings to the mainland may leave you stuck on the island while your flight leaves Athens without you.

THREE

Getting there

None of the islands covered in this book has an airport or plans for one. They are reached by ferry from one of three mainland ports. The prospective traveller must therefore decide which departure point to head for, and from there draft an itinerary if more than one island is to be visited. This chapter aims to provide the information to make this possible.

The mainland — where to head for

Departure point details
● For Andros the port of departure is **Rafina**
● For Kea the departure points are **Lavrion** and **Piraeus** (the latter service may be withdrawn)
● For Kythnos the port of departure is **Piraeus**
● For Serifos the port of departure is **Piraeus**
● For Syros departure points are **Piraeus** and **Rafina**
● For Tinos the departure points are **Piraeus** and **Rafina**

By air to the Greek mainland

The country's main airport is in Athens and although there is a second airport in Thessaloniki to the north, it is unlikely that any of you would use the weekly flight there from London as it is a lot farther away from all the ports.

The airport is situated ten kilometres south of the centre of Athens and the main buildings are divided into what are known as the east main airport and the west main airport — but both use the same runways. The west main airport is used exclusively by Olympic Airways, the Greek national airline, for both overseas and domestic flights. The east main airport is used by all airlines except Olympic.

There are frequent daily flights from both London's Heathrow and Gatwick airports with most of the charter and more inexpensive flights from the latter.

Unless you plan to visit any of the six islands with one of the holiday companies that cover them, your enquiries will be for flight-only details from your local travel agent or from the agencies listed in the low price travel magazines sold in large newsagents.

To enter Greece in this way, regulations demand that you have an accommodation voucher. The companies that sell flight-only seats will provide you with such a voucher for a token payment (e.g. £2). When you receive your tickets, the wallet will also include a confirmation of booking at an address within the mainland. You are not expected to use this address and could find that it is a derelict building if you try to do so.

The flight from London takes approximately three and a half hours and most of the charter flights are at night which are timed nicely to get you to the port in time to watch the sunrise over the docks and then catch the first ferry of the day. Of course you may wish to spend some time on the mainland before moving on but it would really be wiser to plan to see the Acropolis etc. at the end of your holiday; thus if bad weather delays your sailing from the last island at least you would not miss your return flight home.

By rail to the Greek mainland

Greece can be reached by rail from most European countries. From England the cost is surprisingly high and greatly exceeds that of the average budget flight even for those under 26 years of age or who hold a student card. There are daily departures from London's Victoria Station for Athens. A typical journey departs 14.30 hours Monday and arrives at 08.40 hours Thursday having changed trains at Paris and Venice.

— Second class fares (1985): £111.70 single, £239.20 return
— Student and under 26 fares (1985): £89.70 single, £170.30 return
Under 26's are eligible for the Eurorail card that for £115 entitles you to travel on any of Europe's railways for one month. All fares quoted are exclusive of couchette or sleeper facilities for the three night journey.

By coach to the Greek mainland

I have used this form of travel on three occasions and with two different companies. If I were to give the details here, it would be understandable if many of you thought the book had turned into a disaster novel at this point! Probably some passengers actually do have an uneventful journey but it hasn't happened to me yet.

Suffice it to say that meals at the stopping places en route are exorbitantly expensive and that the length of time drivers are willing to spend at toilet stops is quite inadequate (e.g. 5 minutes where there is one toilet and 40 + passengers); so best to take plenty of low fibre food and have a urinary catheter inserted for the three day (they say!) journey! Some drivers will not permit food on board so disguise it.

Details of prices and how to book can be found in the travel and entertainment magazines. At around £35 single, this is by far the cheapest form of travel to Greece. One of the companies now claims to be licensed. You should be aware that a company of this type went bankrupt a few years ago. Of course there are some more reputable firms operating from London to Central Europe but these do not cover Greece. So if ever you book with them to Athens, you may find the second half of your journey is with one of the infamous companies. The reverse is true and on a return journey, I found myself the object of disdain by the driver and courier on the respectable service when they realised who our tickets were with.

A good tip is to take your towel and toiletries onto the ferry where there is a hot shower in the toilets on the upper deck; especially welcome on the return journey.

By ship to the Greek mainland

Most of the remaining international passenger ships calling at Greek ports now operate as cruise liners. Exceptions include some Russian ships operating out of the Black Sea. By far the greater part of passenger capacity is now provided by ubiquitous drive-on/drive-off car ferries. Scheduled services, some sensitive to the Near East political situation, give the following possibilities (+ indicates an increased service in season):

from	between	duration	frequency
Cyprus	Limassol—Piraeus	31-65 hrs	weekly +
Egypt	Alexandria—Piraeus	35-37 hrs	weekly
Israel	Haifa—Piraeus	45-59 hrs	weekly +
Italy	Ancona—Igoumenitsa	23-25 hrs	daily +
	Ancona—Patras	33-36 hrs	daily +
	Bari—Igoumenitsa	12-14 hrs	daily
	Bari—Patras	18 hrs	daily
	Brindisi—Igoumenitsa	9-10 hrs	daily +
	Brindisi—Patras	15-19 hrs	daily +
	Otranto—Igoumenitsa	9 hrs	several weekly
	Venice—Piraeus	39-40 hrs	weekly +
Syria	Latakia—Piraeus	78 hrs	occasional
	Tartous—Volos	(?)	weekly
Turkey	Izmir—Piraeus	(?)	3 x weekly
Yugoslavia	Bar—Igoumenitsa	16 hrs	2 x weekly
	Dubrovnik—Igoumenitsa	18-20 hrs	2 x weekly

By private transport to the Greek mainland

There is no real difficulty in driving across Europe to Greece. The easiest route uses the new toll motorway through Austria from Salzburg to Klagenfurt. The main *autoput* (M1/E94-E5) through Yugoslavia is joined near Ljubljana. It is a flat and uninteresting road crowded with international juggernauts; much has now been reconstructed to full motorway standards, and new sections are regularly added; but parts of the remainder are in dangerously poor condition, especially north of Belgrade. That stretch can be bypassed by taking the M3 south west from Maribor through Osijek to join a good section of the *autoput* near Srem, Mitrovica — a slower but safer and more interesting route.

The coast road down the Adriatic is even more interesting, but 300 kms longer. Being slow and winding, it is also somewhat dangerous. It is not at present possible to transit through Albania, and for political reasons there have sometimes been restrictions on foreign motorists in the province of Kosovo.

Fuel coupons can be bought at the Yugoslav border, for payment in foreign currency. Regulations seem to change in detail from year to year; only recently did it cease to be compulsory for foreigners to use coupons to buy fuel. Currently each coupon has a nominal value of 1300 dinars, but entitles the motorist to an additional 10% of fuel at standard prices (a complex procedure about which some

19

pump attendants feign ignorance). Unused coupons can be refunded at a border, or through the Automobile Association of Yugoslavia (AMSJ) in Belgrade.

The easier way of getting to Greece is to drive down through Italy and take one of the many car ferries listed above. Those sailing from ports in the 'heel' of Italy (Apulia) should give the cheapest overall journey.

Documentation Most English-speaking tourists with valid national passports are entitled to a stay for three months. Their vehicles are even more generously treated, since a 'Carnet de Passage en Douanes' is not necessary for periods of up to four months in Greece: instead, an entry is made in the driver's passport at the frontier. Even after four months, a banker's guarantee is an acceptable alternative to the 'Carnet'. An International Driving Permit is not needed by holders of British and several other European national driving licences. But an insurance 'Green Card', valid for Greece, is mandatory. Entry into Greece will be refused if a passport contains the stamp of the Turkish Republic of Cyprus (Kibris).

Fuel prices (early 1986) The price of Super (96 octane), at 82dr/litre, is comparable with other countries in the area, Regular seems significantly cheaper, but has the very low octane value of 90. Diesel at 48dr/litre, is cheap. There is no price discounting, although fuel prices do vary marginally within the country, depending on distance from the refinery. Currently there is no petrol coupons scheme for tourists.

Motorways The 'motorway' network, classified as National Road, extends from Evzoni on the Yugoslav border to Thessaloniki and Athens, and from Athens to Patras. The greater part is still single carriageway, although some upgrading work is in progress on busier sections. Some stretches of unimproved main road remain. Driving standards are relaxed, although by convention slower-moving traffic drives on the hard shoulder of single carriageways. Between Evzoni and Athens there are at present three toll sections — although another near Thessaloniki can be expected before long — the first near Katerini, and two between Athens and Patras. Charges seem modest to foreigners — for example, about £1 for a private car between Evzoni and Athens. Tickets need to be retained for authentication within each toll section.

Road signs On main roads the road signs invariably appear in pairs. The first shows place names using the Greek alphabet, and is followed at about 100m by a second in the roman alphabet. Numerals of course present no difficulty. All other road signs

20

conform generally to normal European conventions. Turnings off towards camp sites are almost always signposted from the main road.

Breakdowns The Automobile and Touring Club of Greece (ELPA) operates a breakdown service in less remote parts of the country, which is free to foreigners who are members of their own national Automobile or Touring Club. Assistance is obtained by dialling 104.

Sea transport in the Aegean

The only justified criticism of Greek ferry boats is the difficulty in getting accurate information about them. Many shipping companies operate mainland to island services and all are realistic enough to reject the idea of a seasonal timetable. The ships have a habit of occasional over enthusiastic docking which necessitates a month or two in dry dock and juggling with the schedules. (This is a good reason for not standing at the end of the jetty while your ferry comes in!)

The vessels vary in age and size but the majority are large car ferries some of which are ex cross-channel ferries. The service to Kea is of smaller boats that take 6-8 vehicles depending on the size and have only one class of ticket. The larger ships have four classes of passenger in the summer, while in winter everyone buys a third class ticket and sits in the tourist class lounge.

— First class: The standard varies from boat to boat but you are generally paying for seclusion. The fare is about four times that of third class and where there is the choice, works out dearer than flying the same route.

— Second class: Upholstered bench type seats which are comfortable for a snooze. Twice the fare of third class.

— Tourist class: "Pullman" (coach type, reclining) seats in long rows. 50% more expensive than third class.

— Third class: On deck! There are slatted wooden seats and open areas for sunbathing but the decks are grubby and you need something to lie on. (See Sunburn page 50) A few boats have a small lounge for third class passengers. Bear in mind that it gets very cold on board after the sun sets, if you are on a long journey.

Ticket offices On the mainland, particularly in Piraeus, there is always a choice of ticket offices *(practórios)*. Each office represents one or more shipping companies and will deny all knowledge of other companies' sailings. So ask at least three before concluding which is the first departure. Never phrase the question, "Is there a boat to Syros tonight?" — the answer will always be in the affirmative as it is obviously what you want to hear. Just ask when the next ferry leaves for Syros. Prices don't vary from one office to the next but you may be sold a second class ticket if you don't specify. It is possible to buy tickets on board but you never know if someone will be checking them as you get on. There seems to be no pattern to it. Tickets for vehicles are always needed before embarkation. The service from Lavrion to Kea and Kythnos charges 25% extra for tickets bought on board but on all other boats the fare is the same.

Food All the large boats have a restaurant in the second class lounge for the use of all categories of passengers. The food is of reasonable quality and price. However you can't guarantee them opening for evening meals. In the tourist class lounge is a snack bar that sells coffee, beer, soft drinks, snacks, hot pizzas and toast. One of the ferries has the restaurant in the lounge which is not a good idea either for those who are hungry or those who are feeling a bit nauseated.

Other facilities Cabins can be reserved when you buy your ticket but they get full quickly in summer and are suffocatingly hot and stuffy.

You can sometimes change money and travellers cheques at the purser's office, especially if you haven't yet bought a ticket or can point out that you need it to pay for a hot meal; but you would be ill-advised to depend on this.

Despite the fact that most of the men on the islands seem to have spent some time as crew on merchant vessels, the Greeks on the whole are the world's worst sailors and the paper bags start fulfilling their function even before the ship has left port! You may want to bring ear plugs and blindfold if you find the plight of your fellow passengers contagious! For the same reason, the toilets start off in immaculate condition at the beginning of the journey but rapidly deteriorate.

Some ships show videos in the tourist lounge but you have to be sitting near the television to hear the soundtrack as the Greeks rely on the subtitles which can be read from a distance.

Departure points

Piraeus

The country's main port is easily reached from both the centre of Athens and the airport. Not surprisingly it is not a very attractive area and the overall impression is of "grey".

The National Tourist Organisation of Greece prints a free weekly sailing timetable for all ports which can be obtained from their desk in the National Bank of Greece at Syntagma Square or at the east main airport. Because of the size of the port, it is essential to know where your ferry leaves from. Ask when buying your ticket or at the tourist police office inside the electric train station. The small ticket office inside the station is the only one I found that handles all the shipping companies. They speak excellent English and are very helpful. You can't miss it, it is the only one there.

Along the main road, parallel to the dock, are banks, souvenir shops, cafés and *tavernas*. Inside the wire-fenced area of the docks on the corner of the row of ticket offices, is a café that leaves chairs outside all night, thus providing somewhere to wait and watch the sun rise if you have arrived early from a night flight. Transport to Piraeus is fairly good — the journey takes less than an hour.

● From east main airport, Blue Bus No.101 from 05.00 to 22.45 hours every 20 minutes. Opposite the entrance gates to the airport grounds.

● From west main airport, Blue Bus No.107 or 109. By taxi from either airport costs about 450 drachmas but is double at night. Ask before getting in.

● From central Athens, Green Bus No.040 from Filellinon Street (off Syntagma Square), 24-hour service every ten minutes.

● By electric train from Monastiraki, Thission or Omonia Stations in Athens. Trains are every five minutes from 05.00 to 24.00 hours. If you can't find the station, say "traino" to someone and look lost. The fare is 20 drachmas. (See Chapter 8 - Transport)

Rafina

A much more appealing port than Piraeus, it is often suggested that choosing this as a departure point (if you have the option) saves time and money on fares. However these benefits are usually lost in the process of getting there!

● From the airports, you have to take a bus or taxi to the centre of Athens and then walk or take a taxi (if you can get one) to Mavromateon Street at Areos Park, and it is a thirty minute walk.

● From Athens at 29 Mavromateon Street on Areos Park, Orange

Buses leave every 45 minutes from 05.50 to 22.00 hours and more frequently in rush hours on the hour long journey. Luggage goes in the compartment at the side of the bus. Fare 75 drachmas paid inside the bus.

Lavrion

Lavrion is a small port with few facilities. The bus depot is difficult to find if you disembark there. Head for the tree-lined park and it is on the side farthest from the dock. Getting to Lavrion from the airports the route is the same as for Rafina above.

● From Athens, Orange Buses leave from 14 Mavromateon Street hourly from 05.00 to 22.00 hours on the two hour journey. Fare is 155 drachmas.

Island hopping possibilities

The general structure of passenger shipping in the North West Cyclades has already been discussed, and further details are given in Part 2 under the individual islands. But many readers will be interested in planning journeys to other Greek islands by scheduled ferries. Reliable information about some of these is hard to come by, even in Greece. The NTOG issues a weekly sheet covering sailings from all ports. *Greek Travel Pages* and the *Key Travel Guide* can be helpful, but neither is comprehensive. Nor are layout and information easy to understand.

Nevertheless virtually all the islands of any importance now have a car ferry service, relied on as the chief means of bringing in goods, as well as for transporting foot passengers. A few passenger-only ships remain, but the tendency is for them to be replaced by car ferries or hydrofoils. Another trend is for some of the ferries operating from the Athens area to move away from the congestion of Piraeus to smaller ports elsewhere — sometimes also shortening distances.

Where islands lie close to one another, in relation to their distance from the mainland, fairly logical networks have evolved within these groups. But intending passengers should be aware of the following factors:

● The islanders themselves have usually little interest in visiting other islands. Instead they wish to get to the mainland as quickly as possible. This requirement is, of course, opposite to that of the island-hopping tourist, but has had more influence in the planning of schedules.

Syros. Kini. On a quiet Sunday morning a lone fisherman repairs his nets.

● With few exceptions, local operators show little interest in publicising their services. Schedules, where found, probably list sailings by ship rather than the operating company. Destinations are often given as ports, sometimes with obscure names, rather than the islands.

● Shipping companies, all of them privately owned, have their route licences reviewed annually by the Ministry of Mercantile Marine. Whilst established companies are unlikely to be disturbed, more marginal operators bidding for fringe routes may have little idea until late in the previous year which, if any, they are going to be allocated. Bankruptcies, leading to the unexpected halting of services, are not uncommon.

● Modern ferries are required to conform to specifications making them suitable for troop-carrying duties in emergency — the evacuation of PLO fighters from Tripoli in 1983 is an example of this. But hence their apparently casual attitude to passenger comfort in some cases.

● Services between certain Greek islands and the Turkish mainland are very sensitive to tension between the two countries. Sailings may not actually cease, but operators can keep a very low profile — even in departure ports reliable information can be exceptionally hard to obtain. In any event, fares are *very* high in relation to the distances involved; inward and outward bound prices can also vary.

The information contained in the table on following pages has been assembled to assist in the planning of economical island-hopping sequences. It covers only car ferry services; naturally foot passengers, who are free to travel by passenger ships, hydrofoils and caiques, enjoy additional mobility. Islands not listed are either too small, or else motor vehicles cannot be landed there.

Under each island the following information is shown: island ports liable to be given as destinations; normal mainland departure ports; journey times; maximum weekly frequencies; other islands which can be reached directly, as first port of call; international connections. Naturally, since the underlying data are continually changing, confirmation must be obtained locally.

The following example will help to make things clear:

Chios (Eastern Aegean group). Alternative port on the island, Mesta. Mainland departures from Rafina, 7 hours, 3 sailings each week; Piraeus, 10 hours, 6 sailings each week; and Kavalla, 16 hours, 1 sailing each week. From Chios there are direct sailings to Lesbos, 4 hours, more than 7 each week; and to Samos, 3 hours, one each week. There is an international connection to Cesme, 1 hour, frequency at present uncertain.

Key to table

CY = Cyclades. DO = Dodecanese. E = East Aegean. IO = Ionian.
N = North Aegean. SA = Saronic. SP = Sporades.

Numbers in brackets are the approximate duration of journey in hours of the quickest journey. Other numbers are for frequency in high season, whilst f indicates at least 7 services each week.

? indicates there are some doubts as to reliability of data, although some connection is thought probable.

Island destination	Mainland departure	Other islands reached directly	International connections
Aegina (SA) (Ag Marina)	Piraeus (1) f Methana (¾) f	Poros (1¾) f	
Alonissos (SP)	Volos (5½) f Ag. Konstandinos (6) 3 Kimi (2½) 3	Skopelos (½) f	
Amorgos (CY) (Egiali) (Katapola)	Piraeus (?) 4	Paros (3) 1 Astipalea (3) 2 Donoussa (1½) 2 Koufonissia (1) 3	
Anafi (CY)	Piraeus (?) 1	Thera (1) 1	(?cars landed?)
Andros (CY) (Gavrion)	Rafina (3) 6	Tinos (2½) 6 (?)	
Antikythira	Piraeus (18) 2 Gythion (7) 2	Kythira (1) 2 Crete (3) 2	
Astipalea (CY)	Piraeus (?) 2	Amorgos (3) 2 Kalymnos (?) 1 Donoussa (?) 1	
Chios (E) (Mesta)	Piraeus (10) f Kavala (16) 1 Thessaloniki (16) 1	Lesbos (4) f Samos (3) 2 Psara (4½) 4 Dinoussa (1¾) 6	Cesme (1) f
Corfu (IO) (Kerkyra)	Igoumenitsa (1½) f Patras (11½) f	Paxi (2) 3	Brindisi (8) f Bar (13) 2 Bari (10) 6 Dubrovnik (15) 4 Otranto (7) 5+

Island destination	Mainland departure	Other islands reached directly	International connections
Crete			
Chania	Piraeus (11) f		
Heraklion	Piraeus (11½) f	Shinoussa (7) 1	Limassol (27) 2
		Naxos (8) 2	Haifa (43) 2
Kastelli	Gythion (4) 2	Antikythira (3) 2	
Sitia	Kassos (3) 2?		
Folegandros (CY)	Piraeus (?) 1	Sikinos (1) 1	(?cars landed?)
		Thera (3) 1	
Donoussa (CY)	Piraeus (?) 2	Astipalea (?) 1	(?cars landed?)
		Naxos (2) 1	
		Amorgos (2) 2	
Ikaria (E)	Piraeus (10) f	Syros (?) 1	
(Ag. Kirikos)		Paros (4½) 4	
(Evdilos))		Samos (2) f	
Ios (CY)	Piraeus (9) 4	Naxos (2) 4	
		Sikinos (1) 1	
		Thera (3) 4	
Ithaka (IO)	Patras (6) f	Kefallonia (1) f	
(Vathy)	Astakos (2) f	Paxi (5) 1	
(Frikes)	Vassiliki		
Kalymnos (DO)	Piraeus (14) f	Kos (2) f	
		Leros (1½) 5	
		Astipalea (?) 1	
Karpathos (DO)		Kassos (1) 2?	
		Khalki (3) 2?	
Kassos (CO)	Crete (3) 2?		
	Karpathos (1) 2?		
Kea (CY)	Lavrion (1) f	Kythnos (2) 3	
Kefallonia (IO)	Killini (1½) f	Ithaka (1) f	Brindisi (14) 3
(Poros)	?Patras (3½) f	Zakinthos (2) 1	
(Sami)	Igoumenitsa (5) 3		
(Fiskardo)	Vassiliki (1½) f		
	Astakos (3½) f		
Khalki (DO)		Karpathos (3) 2?	
		Rhodes (3) 2?	
Kimolos (CY)	Piraeus (11) 2	Milos (2) 2	
		Syros (4) 2	
		Sifnos (2) 1	

Island destination	Mainland departure	Other islands reached directly	International connections
Kythira (Ag. Pelagia) (Kapsali) (Platia Ammos)	Piraeus (11) 2 Neapolis (1) 5 Gythion (2½) 2	Nil	
Kythnos (CY)	Lavrion (2) 3 Piraeus (3½) 4	Serifos (2) 4 Kea (2) 3	
Kos (DO)	Piraeus (16) f	Kalymos (2) 6 Rhodes (4½) 6 Nissiros (?) 1	Bodrum (½) ?
Koufonissia (CY)	Piraeus (?) 3	Shinoussa (1) 3 Amorgos (1) 3	
Lemnos (E) (Myrina) (Kastro)	Kavala (5) 4 Piraeus (?) 1 Ag.K'standinos (10) 1 Kimi (5½) 1	Lesbos (6) f Ag. Efstratios (2) 2	
Leros (DO)	Piraeus (12) 5	Kalymnos (1½) 5 Patmos (1½) 5	
Lesbos (E) (Mytilini)	Kavala (14) 2 Piraeus (13) f Thessaloniki (16) 1	Chios (4) f Lemnos (6) f	Dikeli (2) ?
Milos (CY)	Piraeus (9) 3	Kimolos (2) 2 Sifnos (2) 3	
Mykonos (CY)	Piraeus (?) 3 Rafina (?) 5?	Tinos (?) f?	(?cars landed?)
Naxos (CY)	Piraeus (6) f	Paros (1) f Crete (8) 2 Donoussa (1½) 1 Ios (2) 4	
Nissiros (DO)	Piraeus (?) 1	Kos (?) 1 Tilos (?) 1	(?cars landed?)
Oinoussa (E)		Chios (1¾) 6	
Paros (CY)	Rafina (5½) 3 Piraeus (6½) f	Ikaria (4½) 4 Amorgos (?) 1 Naxos (1) f Syros (2) f	

Island destination	Mainland departure	Other islands reached directly	International connections
Patmos (DO)	Piraeus (10) 5	Leros (1½) 5 Syros (?) 1	
Paxi (10)	Patras (10) 1	Corfu (2) 3 Ithaca (5) 1	
Poros (SA)	Methana (½) f Piraeus (3) f Galatas (5 mins) f	Aegina (1¾) f	
Psara (E)		Chios (4½) 4	
Rhodes (DO)	Piraeus (15+) f	Khalki (3) 2? Kos (4½) 6 Symi (?) 1	Limassol (14) 4 Marmaris (2) Latakia (55) 1 Haifa (28) 1 Alexandria (39) 1
Salamis (SA)	Perama (10 mins) f Perama (Megara) (¼) f	Nil	
Samos (E) (Vathy) (Karlovasi)	Piraeus (12) f	Ikaria (2) f Chios (3) 2	Kusadasi (2) f
Samothraki (N) Karala (4) 1	Alexandrou-polis (3) f	Nil	
Serifos (CY)	Piraeus (5) 4	Kithnos (2) 4 Sifnos (1) 2	
Shinoussa (CY)	Piraeus (?) 3	Crete (?) 3 Koufonissia (?) 3	(?cars landed?)
Sifnos (CY) (Apollonia)	Piraeus (6) 4	Milos (2) 3 Serifos (1) 4 Kimolos (2) 1	
Sikinos (CY)	Piraeus (?) 1	Ios (1) 1 Folegandros (1) 1	(?cars landed?)
Skiathos (SP)	Volos (3) f Ag. K'dinos (3) f Kimi (4½) 3	Skopelos (1) f Lemnos ?	
Skiros (SP)	Kimi (2) f	Ag.Efstratios (4)?	

Island destination	Mainland departure	Other islands reached directly	International connections
Skopelos (SP)	Volos (4) f Ag. K'dinos (4) f Kimi (3½) 3	Alonissos (½) f Skiathos (1) f	
Symi (DO)	Piraeus (?) 1	Tilos (?) 1 Rhodes (?) 1 Patmos (?) 1	
Syros (CY)	Piraeus (4½) f Rafina (3½) 3	Ikaria (4½) 1 Kimolos (4) 1 Paros (2) f Tinos (1) f	
Thassos (N) (Prinos)	Kavala (1) f Keramoti (½) f	Nil	
Thera (CY) (Santorini) (Oia)	Piraeus (12) 5	Anafi (2) 1 Ios (3) 4 Folegandros (3) 1	
Tilos (DO)	Piraeus (?) 1	Nissiros (?) 1 Symi (?) 1	(?cars landed?)
Tinos (CY)	Rafina (5½) 6 Piraeus (?) 3	Andros (2½) 6 Mykonos (1) f? Syros (1) 4	
Zakinthos (10)	Killini (1) f	Kefallonia (2) 1	

Note. Euboea and Levkas, both technically islands, but with bridge or chain-ferry road connection, have been treated as if part of the mainland

FOUR

Accommodation

All the islands have a variety of accommodation available, to be found predominantly in the main town and to a lesser extent the other centres of population. Names of hotels with category, telephone number and location are listed in the individual island chapters.

What to expect

The local tourist police and N.T.O.G. allocate a category for all rooms to let both in private houses and hotels. This is decided by the standard and amount of facilities available. Something like a telephone in the room can upgrade it from a C to a B. The standard varies from one island to another and of the islands covered by this book, Syros and Kea are the most expensive; but to put it in proportion, this means paying about an extra £1 per night there.

One characteristic of Greek rooms is that they are smaller than you may be used to and although the furniture is kept to a minimum it is often necessary to organise a one-way system around the room! Another is that the sheets seem to have been carefully measured to exactly fit the top of the bed with no allowance for tucking in at the bottom, top or sides! If you are used to more than one pillow, improvisation is called for.

Conventional baths are about as rare in Greece as Turks, and showers are the norm. Some islands experience a shortage of water in the summer and many water heating systems use solar panels, which means that your shower will be hotter at night than in the morning. Some have electrical back-up for the winter and the controls look like a fuse box with a round knob bearing "O" and "I" symbols. You may be allowed to turn on the water heater yourself but many Greeks seem to believe that these controls are beyond the understanding of most tourists! Towels and soap are provided.

The room category and basic and extras charges are shown on an official card usually displayed behind the door. The prices shown are the maximum the owner is allowed to charge by law but if business is slack he may be willing to accept less. If the room charge does not include the price of showers, this will also be shown on the card, so look here for otherwise hidden extras.

The various categories are: Luxury (sky's the limit!); A 2,900 — 5,000 drachmas; B 2,450 — 3,700 drachmas; C 1,200 — 2,200 drachmas; D 850 — 1,300 drachmas; E 600 — 900 drachmas.

The prices quoted are a rough guide only and apply to a double room in high season.

On most of the islands, people meet the ferries and cries of "Rooms, rooms" indicate their purpose. This practice is illegal but tolerated. The hotel and room representatives judge the new arrival by his/her appearance and approach those they think most suited to their accommodation. Many establishments run mini buses to transport you from the port to your room.

Camping

It is strictly illegal to sleep on beaches with or without camping equipment but, except for town beaches, the police turn a blind eye until prompted into action by local hotel and room owners. If all official accommodation becomes full (as it can) then sleeping under the stars is permitted as long as no fire of any kind is started either deliberately or accidentally. If you do start a fire, you are automatically provided with free accommodation for a minimum of two months in a Greek prison!

Camping grounds are a rarity and seldom meet the demand. The authorities are now providing financial aid to those who plan to build camp sites but as they require a large plot of land and must have a high standard of facilities, they are still a costly venture.

FIVE

Food, drink and leisure activities

Food

Most people will have eaten in a Greek restaurant in their home country at least once. If you have ever ordered *mezedes* you will have a good idea of the character of Greek food as it consists of a little of most of the dishes on the menu. Because most of the Greek restaurants in the U.K. are Cypriot owned, there will be slight variations in flavourings and of course the selection may be more limited by the difficulty in obtaining fresh ingredients, such as octopus and squid, which are readily available in Greece.

One major difference however will be the temperature of the food. In Greece it is unusual to find dishes served hotter than warm. This is not due to poor service or lack of facilities but is the way Greek people are used to serving and eating their food.

Centuries ago, each village had a central kitchen where the food was prepared for the entire community and a member of each family would take the appropriate containers to the kitchen and return with the family's share of the food at meal times. On the way home, the food would cool considerably and this is said to be the reason why they developed the habit of eating luke-warm meals.

Because not many Greek kitchens have an oven, just hot plates, you can often see the women taking containers of food ready for cooking to the bakers shop where, for a small fee, their cakes or joint of meat are cooked for them.

Breakfast The Greek people do not place much importance on breakfast and the N.T.O.G. is at present encouraging hotels to offer an alternative to the "continental breakfast" that consists of tea or coffee, toast, butter, jam and sometimes a piece of madeira cake.

Many cafés advertise "English breakfast"; however, if you

choose sausages with your eggs, you will find them very "un-English" and more like little spicy frankfurters, tasty nevertheless. The ham is rather like salami but the bacon is what we are used to and of a high quality.

Most cafés use evaporated milk in coffee which is always called "Nescafé" to distinguish it from Greek coffee (it will be instant, though not necessarily that particular brand). Also, you can expect to have hot milk to go with your morning cup of tea! The butter is unsalted and the apricot marmalade bears a striking resemblance to apricot jam (delicious).

Tavernas
They vary in standard and prices but generally serve inexpensive traditional dishes which you select by going into the kitchen and pointing at what you want. This is an excellent way of ensuring that you like the look of what you order and of overcoming any language problems, although most owners and waiters speak at least enough English to cover all eventualities in their work. Only a very few *tavernas* serve desserts or coffee and you are expected to go elsewhere for "afters".

Restaurants
Their main difference from *tavernas* is that they are open at lunch time as well as in the evening and generally have a larger selection of food that may include steaks and some French and English dishes. They may also provide a small selection of desserts, coffee and after dinner drinks.

Zaharoplastéons
These cake shops sell gateaux, pastries and yoghourt to eat on the premises or take away. Coffee, tea, soft drinks, liqueurs and spirits are served but never wine or beer. It is to these shops you come for the sweet course of your meal and after dinner drinks. They generally keep shop hours.

Cafeniōns
All types of alcohol, soft and hot drinks are sold with a small selection of cakes.

Ouzerías
The Greek men (especially those whose working life is over) spend a large part of each day in a café or *ouzeria* watching the world go by or discussing politics, emphasising each point with energetic

35

hand gestures and raised voices. The latter is often confused by foreigners as a sign of a heated row in progress but this doesn't follow in Greece. A friendly but enthusiastic conversation can often include the participants yelling at each other!

On offer you will find Nescafé and Greek coffee, *ouzo, Metaxa* cognac, beer, soft drinks and a few pastries. If you order *ouzo* or cognac, be sure to order some *mezes* which complement the drinks. They are small plates of tomato, cucumber, bread with *tsatsiki, taramasalata* and anchovies and, of course, olives. At about twenty drachmas, it is also excellent value.

If you are watching the sunset from one of these establishments, you will be able to enjoy some of the grilled octopus that is served at this time of day. The octopus have to be tenderised which explains why people can be seen apparently taking out a bad temper on the unresisting (lifeless) octopus. They are then hung up to dry in the sun so watch your head as you walk under the awnings! Small pieces of the grilled tentacles are served on sticks with lemon juice and it is customary to drink the remaining juice from the saucer, it is also the best bit in my opinion! Don't be put off by its appearance, it is delicious.

Menus

A popular source of tourist entertainment are the bilingual menus found in all eating places. The variety of spelling mistakes can be hilarious and it is occasionally impossible to work out what they are trying to say. I can recommend "roast staff" from a *taverna* in Syros. Presumably one of the waiters fell foul of the chef! (Perhaps you would like to send me any howlers you find for inclusion in future editions).

Although the menus are lengthy, only the dishes with prices beside them are available. The two prices for each dish are with and without tax. It is usual to leave a 10% tip divided between the waiter and boy who brought the bread and drinks.

Meat When you look at the dishes on offer in the kitchen, the meat will probably look as if it died of old age and has been dried out even more in the cooking. Don't you believe it! If the cook can manage to get it on to the plate before it disintegrates, you will see how deceptive appearances can be.

Fish and shell fish In fish tavernas you choose your fish from a refrigerated display cabinet and it is then cooked for you. Price is by weight and is not as cheap as you might expect.

Drinks

Greek coffee This is similar to Turkish coffee but I don't suggest you order it as such. It comes with varying amounts of sugar and is always served black in a *demi-tasse* with a glass of cold water. Never stir it and beware of the considerable amount of sediment in the bottom. You drink it: without sugar — *skéto;* with a little sugar — *médrio;* incredibly sweet — *gleekó.*

Retsina Wine containers used to be made of hide treated with tree sap or resin. This flavoured the contents and the Greeks developed a taste for it this way and so today they add resin to some of the many local wines purely for the taste. This is definitely an acquired taste but at 45 drachmas a bottle, some feel the incentive to acquire it!

When drinking any alcoholic beverage in Greece, it is customary to chink glasses before drinking and with each refill. The origin of this custom is said to be that the Gods decreed that wine should please all five senses. The only one not obviously satisfied was hearing, hence chinking glasses.

Wine Those of you who enjoy being able to expound on which end of which vineyard the grapes came from for each glass of vintage French wine, may be a little disappointed in the Greek wines. Very few if any eating places on the islands covered stock imported wines although there can be a large selection of the local produce. My own preference is for the rosé wines but I have never been noted for having a refined palate.

Beer At least four different brands of beer are sold in Greece. *Fix* is a local brew and *Amstel* is produced in Greece under licence from Holland. They are all lager type beers and are sold by the litre. Bottle sizes are half litre which is roughly three quarters of a pint for 50 drachmas. Draught lager is new to the islands but catching on fast.

Ouzo An aniseed flavoured spirit that is clear until water is added at which time it turns a milky white.

Cognac Locally produced brandies are slightly sweeter than those produced in France but are enjoyable and at 25 drachmas a time, very inexpensive. Duty free bottled five star Greek brandy works out at a ludicrous £1.60 for 750 mls.

Raki Sometimes known as *souma* this colourless spirit is very popular with the locals. The taste and more particularly the aroma varies greatly. One I tried had such a revolting smell that try as I might, I couldn't get it near enough to taste it.

Drink (and food) prices are all dictated by the tourist police who consider the facilities available before setting the price, e.g. beer is always 50 drachmas in a *cafenión* but may be 100 drachmas in a bar and 150 in a discotheque. The local businessmen on my home island of Paros recently went on strike for two days bemoaning the price fixing level. It hasn't made any difference however and they lost £50,000 per day in takings.

The Greeks never seem to suffer the day after a heavy drinking session and this is probably due to the fact that large glasses of cold water are served with all spirits and they never drink without taking a little food at the same time.

Entertainment

The variety of nightlife on each island is of course proportional to the extent of its involvement in the tourist industry.

Discotheques
These places vary greatly from an improvised dance floor in the middle of a field to fairly sophisticated night spots. The disc jockeys seemed to be picked for fairness of face rather than musical knowledge or technique and generally have a complete disregard for whether anyone else is enjoying the music. Not all discotheques have an admission charge but where they do, it will include the price of your first drink. The cheapest way to get round the higher drink prices is to buy a bottle of wine and share it.

Bars
In summer, most bars have seats outside where it is possible to talk above the music played.

Bazoukis
There is never an admission charge but the price of drinks can be phenomenal, e.g. 800 drachmas for a gin and tonic. Some *bazoukis* only serve whisky to drink and most have a large selection of food including the speciality of fruit salad — popular since it is usually the cheapest thing on the menu. Live Greek music is played by a group of at least six musicians and one or more of them will sing. The locals tend to get very enthusiastic on an evening at the *bazouki* and the plates inevitably start being shattered on the dance floor as a gesture of appreciation.

Greek dancing

I don't think it is possible not to enjoy watching the local men dancing, at least on the first occasion. Whether it is a single old timer dancing because he just can't help himself or a group of young lads out to impress the girls, you can't help being caught up in the atmosphere it creates and the skill involved. By all means clap along to the music but lone females should realise the significance of crouching at the edge of the dance floor and clapping on their own to a male dancing, as in some places it implies a very intimate relationship. You might prefer to watch the dancing in a bar or disco rather than a *bazouki* where it tends to get too crowded to be able to see what is happening. Many bars have someone used to teaching tourists the steps and they have a strange knack of conveying what you are supposed to do next even if not in words.

Cinemas

Many islands have open air cinemas that add an extra dimension to watching old movies. Most films shown in the summer are in English with Greek subtitles. Comedies are less suitable than thrillers or westerns as the locals often read the subtitles and start laughing, preventing you from hearing the punch line in the dialogue.

Sailing

Tinos is the only island covered that has sailing boats for hire but it may be possible to make arrangements to hire privately owned vessels from locals or resident expatriates.

Flotilla holidays There are a small number of mainland companies which organise flotilla holidays. The selection of islands to be visited is often decided by the consensus of opinion among the passengers; and so you may see a large number of sailing boats moored in the harbour. Be warned that they can be moored there for six months or more as, in the past, the island port police have declared the boats to carry inadequate safety equipment and have impounded them for eventual auction to cover the mooring fees and fines. This of course left the unfortunate holidaymakers stranded, so check out the company first if you plan to use this method of getting about.

A less strenuous way of tenderising octopus. The younger men dash them against the rocks.

Beaches

Most Greek beaches are thoroughly cleared of seaweed and litter at the start of the season. One of the reasons why sleeping on the beaches is opposed is because of the human waste and rubbish that has been left there to spoil the enjoyment of others in the past. Enough said.

Tinos and Syros have windsurfers and water skiing equipment for hire and tuition from their most popular beaches.

Swimming

One of the joys of the beaches is that swimming is safe for both adults and children, as undercurrents and undersea shelves are very rare indeed. Swimming is an enjoyable part of most people's holiday both because of the need to cool off intermittently when sunbathing and because the Aegean has an enticing variety of all the shades of blue and green imaginable, that proves irresistible to young and old alike. Many beaches are bordered by rocky outcrops where snorkellers can explore the variety of marine life found there.

In the shallows, if you stay still long enough, tiny transparent fish, with markings on the tail that look like eyes at the other end, will gently nibble at your legs possibly to remove the grains of salt that the evaporating seawater leaves.

Nudism

The Greek people do not understand the joys of swimming and sunbathing naked or even topless. On my home island, the locals have been prompted into printing notices reminding people that it is illegal and suggesting where they should go to prevent causing offence. Where idiotic individuals have been callous enough to peel off on town beaches, you will find mothers feel obliged to take an alternative route home with school children.

All the islands have at least one beach suitable for nudism so it is no hardship to show some consideration for your hosts. Many holidays have been spoilt when offenders were taken to court, fined and had their passports endorsed to prevent subsequent re-entry to the country. The police have been known to don swimming trunks and to look for naturists before returning in uniform to make the arrests.

Diving

A new law has been introduced that forbids the use of air tanks for diving unless a permit is held by the diver. This is to prevent the removal of antiquities and damage to unexcavated archaeological sites on the sea bottom.

IMPORT AND EXPORT OF ANTIQUES

Antiquities may be imported into Greece free of duty, provided they are declared on entry by the owner; failing this, they will be regarded as having been acquired in Greece and their re-export will be banned. Antiquities imported into Greece and declared at Customs may be re-exported free of any other formality.

Antiquities may be taken out of the country only on a special permit issued by the Ministry of Culture and Science. The Greek state has the right to prohibit the export of any one antique object, in which case, if the interested party seeks its exportation the state is under obligation to purchase the antique in question for half the price declared by the exporter. Any attempt to carry out of the country illegally items of antique value is liable to prosecution. Moreover, any person found guilty of assisting in the illegal export of any antique object is considered an accomplice and is liable to prosecution.

PURCHASE AND EXPORT OF COPIES OF ANTIQUITIES

There is a permanent exhibition of frescoes, plaster casts and copies of various masterpieces found in museums all over Greece, in the National Archaeological Museum of Athens. The objects on display are for sale and can be exported without any formality.

The accessibility of Greece's rich heritage of antiquities has always proved tempting to collectors and souvenir hunters. The Greek state now has strict controls to prevent antique works being taken out of the country illegally and penalties for infringement are severe.

SIX

Shopping

Shop opening hours

Like all the times quoted in this chapter, these must be taken as a guide only, but in general they are 08.00 to 13.00 hours and 17.00 to 20.00 hours Monday to Saturday, with no evening opening on Mondays and Wednesdays. Souvenir shops and boutiques may not bother to close in the afternoon and may be open on Sundays and late into the evening depending on the number of potential buyers on the streets. Most shops close for the various religious holidays and in addition to these, shops have their own name days (see page 57) according to the type of shop. No warning is posted, even in Greek, of these holidays to enable you to stock up on food, etc.

What to buy

Everyone has different ideas about which souvenirs are tasteful or gawdy but Greece has a large selection of the former. Practical cheesecloth dresses, attractive ceramics, handmade jewellery, fringed scarves, dazzling posters and postcards, leather shoes, brassware and statuettes are just some of the souvenirs that are worth buying for reasons other than purely as a holiday memento. Particular bargains are: Greek cigarettes, cognac, wines, suntan oil, cheesecloth dresses and silver jewellery.

Comparative sizes
● Shoe sizes

English	3	4	5	6	7	8	9	10	11
Greek	35½	37	38	39½	40½	42	43	44	45½

● Bust sizes						
English	32	34	36	38	40	42	44
Greek	81	86	91	97	102	107	112

● Dress sizes						
English	8	10	12	14	16	18
Greek	36	38	40	42	44	46

Weight

Almost everything in Greece is sold by weight in kilos, including string, wine, paper and nails: 1 kilo = 2.2 lb.

What to bring

There are few things that cost significantly more in Greece to make it worth bringing them from home. Photographic film is marginally cheaper at home and black and white film is almost impossible to find in Greece. If you plan to be self-catering, beef stock cubes, coffee whitener and bran are about the only things not available at the supermarkets. Double the cost in Greece are paperback books and I consequently enter a plea on behalf of Greek island resident expatriates who would dearly love to get their hands on some fresh reading material. Don't throw books and newspapers away, try and find someone to give them to or persuade your hotel to start a small library.

Books and newspapers

All the islands covered by this book stock English paperbacks and newspapers in summer but it is possible that on Andros the only paper available may be the *Athens News*. Newspaper prices vary according to the weight and published price of the paper, 85-120 drachmas. Some glossy magazines are available on the larger islands but the prices are the same as for a typical paperback at 600 to 750 drachmas.

The Athens News The Greek-produced English language daily covers world news, sport and TV and radio details. The emphasis is on Greek news and it always gives details of who the Prime Minister had lunch with! In tabloid form with fairly conservative looking format, this newspaper has some occasionally outrageous articles, e.g. ''Rapists spit roasted before being fed to snakes'', and the reports of family vendettas in Crete are pretty amazing.

Post Office

Post offices *(Taheedroméeo)* are easily distinguished by their bright yellow sign posts with black lettering. The same colour scheme is found on the post boxes. Opening hours are from 07.30 to 14.00 hours, larger branches may stay open for an additional half hour; closed Saturdays and Sundays. All post offices on the smaller islands and the main post office on the larger islands provide a Poste Restante service. Passports must be presented when collecting letters and parcels. There may be some confusion over which letter of the Greek alphabet your post has been filed under, so ask anyone writing to you to use only your Christian and surname and to underline the surname. This avoids the possibility of it being filed under Mr or Mrs.

Postage stamps can sometimes be bought at shops selling postcards. They are allowed to charge 10% above the face value of the stamps.

Telephone Offices

The abbreviation for the Greek name for these offices is O.T.E. pronounced owtay. Every island has at least one but they vary from large buildings to someone's spare room! International calls and local calls can be made from here but local calls are not allowed from the O.T.E.'s in Athens, you must use a kiosk.

The 'phone booth contains a meter and a table to tell you the cost of various meter readings, e.g. 100 units = 290 drachmas. The length of time for each unit depends, of course, on where you are calling. Before dialling, the meter must be at zero. The assortment of noises made by the telephone system is very different from ours. The ringing tone at first sounds like our engaged tone but the notes are coupled and have a long pause between couples.

When your call is completed, you pay at the desk having indicated which booth you have used. A receipt will be given. Opening hours 08.00 to 14.30 hours and 17.30 to 21.00 hours Monday to Friday, half day only Saturday; but these hours vary enormously from island to island.

Transfer charge and person to person calls will be placed for you but it may entail waiting in the office for up to two hours. **Telegrams** These offices also handle telegrams but it is always cheaper to telephone.

Telephone kiosks

Kiosks with blue or orange bands at the top of the sides. The blue ones use ten drachma coins which must be inserted before dialling but after lifting the receiver. The orange booths can take international calls and use ten, twenty and 50 drachma coins. A tiny dim red light goes on a split second before you get cut off and there are no pips to tell you to put in more money. Unused coins should be returned to you when you replace the receiver but this system is as prone to faults as our own. None of the kiosks takes incoming calls. Very little vandalism of 'phone boxes is found in Greece.

The kiosks known as *peripteros* (see page 48) have metered 'phones from where you can make local or international calls but each unit is four drachmas compared to 2.9 at the O.T.E. It is possible to get people to ring you back here as long as the owner doesn't mind.

Banks and currency

Banks

Serifos and Kea do not have banks as such but on Kea a shop-keeper in the capital is an official agent. On Serifos the hotels and ticket offices take travellers cheques and Eurocheques but I suggest you try and avoid having to rely on this by getting the maximum amount of drachmas from your local bank and changing as much as you will need for those islands when you arrive in Greece. Your passport is needed for all transactions.

If you plan to stay longer than three months in Greece, save the pink exchange slips as you will need them when applying for a visa renewal.

Opening hours are from 08.00 to 13.30 hours (13.00 Friday) Monday to Friday. Where a large number of tourists are found, the banks may stay open later and may even open on Saturdays for exchange only. These hours will be displayed outside the bank. Some Greek banks have been on strike on and off for the last year but an exchange desk remains open.

Currency

The exchange rate for sterling varies from day to day but over the last year it has only wavered within a ten drachma per pound margin and is about the same now as twelve months ago. (1986: £1 = 263 drachmas.)

Bank notes These come in increasing size according to value, and in various colours. Denominations are: 50 drachmas (light blue); 100 drachmas (pinky red); 500 drachmas (green); 1,000 drachmas (brown); and 5,000 drachmas (navy).

The newly introduced 5,000 drachma notes are very difficult to change and if you offer one to pay for a packet of cigarettes, the shopkeeper might well become hysterical. On the subject of shopkeepers, it is easier to understand their being reluctant to give change when you realise that Greek banks will not provide bags of coins: a year ago there was only one coin counting machine in the whole country!

Coins These are also in increasing size according to value. Denominations are: one drachma (bronze); two drachmas (bronze); five drachmas (silver); ten drachmas (silver); twenty drachmas (silver); and fifty drachmas (silver).

The fifty drachma coins are new and, although larger, can be easily confused with the twenty drachma coin, so be careful.

Supermarket prices may have two figures after a decimal point. This is because the drachma is theoretically divided into a hundred lepta. No lepta coins exist and this is just a way of inching up prices.

Kiosks

Found on most street corners these orangy brown painted constructions are known as *peripteros* in Greek. Somehow they manage to stock a larger selection of goods than most Woolworths, including cigarettes, matches, sweets, nuts, chocolate, razors, pens, contraceptives, aspirins, vapour rub, throat sweets, newspapers, books, magazines, maps, adhesive tape, paper, envelopes and a multitude of other things. Most have a metered telephone for public use.

The occupants are often disabled or war veterans as kiosks are State allocated. Opening hours vary but many only close from midnight to 07.00 hours.

SEVEN

Your health and comfort

Medical care

All of the islands covered by this book have at least one doctor. On smaller islands, the doctor is probably newly trained and doing a form of community work in lieu of his National Service. The location of surgeries is mentioned under the Useful Addresses section of each island chapter. In some places the surgeries double as the only pharmacy. Opening hours are posted outside. In case of serious illness, patients are transported by boat or helicopter to the nearest hospital.

Theoretically if you obtain form E.111 from an office of the Department of Health and Social Security (see leaflet S.A.30) before leaving the U.K., you will be entitled to treatment at a token cost. In practice, the problems of getting the necessary forms completed by the doctor make this a nonsense. A consultation will cost approximately 1,000 drachmas.

General health

It is not necessary to have any inoculations before visiting Greece unless you have recently visited an area where yellow fever or cholera are endemic.

The main health problem you may encounter is from the laxative properties of the olive oil, which forms an ingredient for almost everything except bread! A change of diet has the same effect, so don't rush to the chemist for antibiotics at the first sign of gastric disturbances. A kaolin mixture or Lomotil taken after each bowel movement gives speedy relief and can be purchased from local chemists without prescription. Remember to maintain an adequate fluid and salt intake or you could get some painful stomach cramps.

49

Medical insurance

Medical insurance to cover accidents and emergency treatments is recommended for travellers to Greece. Remember that there are few hospitals in the islands and should you need hospital treatment the costs of being transported there — even apart from the treatment itself — could be very high indeed. Your travel agent will give you the latest information about insurance policies. Check that the sum you are insured for is adequate. Emergency surgery such as an appendectomy, for example, can be very costly. If you were unfortunate to need anything like this, it would also delay your return home — so make sure that the medical insurance you take out is realistic.

Hazards

Greece is the home of a few nasties including small white scorpions, black widow and brown hermit spiders plus two species of poisonous snakes. You are extremely unlikely to encounter any of these little treasures whose venom is rarely fatal. Should you be unlucky enough to be bitten or stung, don't try to imitate anything you may have seen in the movies as this only speeds up the spread of the venom. Get help as quickly as possible giving a description of what "got you".

There are no strong currents or undercurrents on the island beaches and the only hazards are sea urchins and jellyfish, both of which are painful. Leave sea urchin spines alone, trying to get them out only pushes them further in. Apply some olive oil and keep pressure off the affected area, they will work their own way out. Jellyfish can sting even when dead and beached, so if you find one why not move it out of harm's way with a stick, as other people may not be as observant as you.

Sunburn

There is one very serious danger lurking for the unprotected: the sun. The gentle breeze is very pleasant but it masks the strength of the sun. This is particularly true on the sundecks of the ferries, where you can relax comfortably for long enough to start your holiday with third degree burns. Sun screens and after-sun creams are available more cheaply than at home and with a mind-boggling selection. Take sunbathing slowly at first, Greek dancing becomes agony with sunburnt shoulders! Whatever you do, never fall asleep in the sun.

Toilets

Greek toilets are not the sort of places in which you would want to spend any length of time. Most are of the type we are used to but some are the "squatting" variety. In the latter be careful of losing the contents of your pockets. In all toilets, a basket or bin is provided into which you must put all used toilet paper as the plumbing can't cope with it. To operate the flush, push the plunger underneath the cistern.

Men's and women's toilets are differentiated by the usual trousered and skirted figures on the doors. A single toilet usually bears the letters "W.C.".

Public toilets are rare but all eating places have to have them by law. Only a few will insist that they are for the use of customers only. The Greek word for toilet is pronounced *too allétta*.

Drinking water

The water is safe to drink in all parts of Greece but the taste varies. On Syros it is very briny and fresh water is sold by street vendors. Bottled water is available at all supermarkets for about 35 drachmas for 1½ litres. These plastic bottles are useful for taking to the beach (and light to bring back to town for disposal!).

The water generally has a high concentration of minerals and a photographer friend tells me that he finds it impossible to get any of his developing chemicals to dissolve in it.

EIGHT

Getting about

Time and distance

Greek time is one or two hours ahead of that in England depending on the time of year. This is not the only difference, as the whole concept of time bears no similarity to our own. Expressions such as morning, midday, afternoon and evening are so flexible as to be meaningless. If you are trying to make an appointment of any kind, specify the exact hour and even then, unless you say "English time", rendezvous will be anything up to two hours later or "Greek time".

Distance is equally flexible and "near", "just around the corner" and "a few minutes walk" can turn out to be a few kilometres.

Transport

Taxis In the centre of Athens it is very difficult to get a taxi even though these bright yellow cars account for about 50% of the traffic. The problem is caused by the regulations introduced to lessen smog in the city, which stipulate that vehicles may only be used on alternate days according to the registration numbers. Consequently car owners must find an alternative method of getting to work — and they appropriate the taxis.

Taxi ranks at Syntagma Square, underground stations and both airports are some good places to try. Otherwise you have to stand somewhere where the occupied taxis are forced to slow down or stop, traffic lights for example, and shout your destination through the window. Each passenger will pay the full fare unless you are travelling together therefore picking up single passengers rather than a couple is more lucrative.

On all of the islands, the taxis are metallic grey.

Buses On the islands, buses have a relaxed atmosphere and it doesn't matter which door you use to get in. On the mainland the pace of life is that much faster and you have to get in at the front and pay the exact fare into a box near the driver. If you don't know the fare, have plenty of change handy. Keep the ticket as many routes are checked on every journey by an inspector.

There is no uniformity in the appearance of bus stop signs and so you just have to watch where people get on.

On the islands, all the buses are a mid blue unless otherwise stated.

Trains Operating only in Athens and its suburbs, is a single route electric train. These trains mostly run above ground from Kifissia to Piraeus and are useful for getting from Athens to Piraeus. The fare is 20 drachmas, 40 drachmas maximum for longer journeys. Ticket offices don't open until about 08.00 and so if the man in the office is ignoring you, just walk through the turnstile and tickets will not be checked at the other end. Later in the day you must buy a valid ticket from either the machines or office and retain it for inspection at the other end.

Pedestrians Crossing the road in Athens takes either nerves of steel or suicidal tendencies. They have plenty of red and green men to advise you but the trouble is that when the green man is lit, it only means that traffic wishing to go straight ahead is being shown a red light. Where drivers can turn right, they may still have a green light and so you have to dodge them.

There seems to be no penalty for parking on the zebra crossing while waiting for the lights to change and you often have to pick your way around and squeeze between vehicles on the striped area.

Motorbike and moped rental

The majority of the bikes have seen better days and survived some rough treatment that the mechanics have a knack of camouflaging with a coat of paint. Some important points to remember when hiring a vehicle:-

● Make sure it works! Take it for a test drive which will also —
● Ensure that you can handle it.
● Negotiate the price, especially if hiring for more than one day. Does the price include petrol.
● Get the 'phone number of the agency in case of breakdown. All of them have their own breakdown trucks and they don't sit idle for long.

● Seriously consider asking for one of their crash helmets. At no extra charge, these look like multi-coloured tortoises and while they won't do a thing to improve your image they may prove to be your salvation: there are so many "holidaydrivers" around in the summer that even if *you* know what you are doing, you may fall foul of someone else who doesn't. Accidents are literally an everyday occurrence. Most people get away with cuts and bruises but every time you see that helicopter overhead, someone has been badly injured and is on his way to the hospital.

● Make a firm arrangement about returning the bike. The expression used may be "for the day" but if you return a bike after 19.00 hours, you will find yourself unpopular with the employee who has had to work late for you. If you want to keep it until the next morning, make it clear.

● Be sure you take notice of the traffic signs (the same as in Europe). Many of the roads are closed to motorbikes and mopeds even though cars are permitted. Keep your eyes open and don't forget that they drive on the right hand side in Greece!

● Where island roads are of a poor standard, choose a bike with large wheels.

● Resist the temptation to take corners at speed.

If your bike does break down and your knowledge of their mechanical workings is limited or non-existent, try taking the petrol cap off and then rocking the bike from side to side to hear if you have got any petrol left (petrol = *vin zeé nee)*. Have a look for the sparkplug which is usually found between the front wheel (that round thing) and a grooved thing the size of a small loaf of bread that burns your fingers when you touch it. If you locate the sparkplug make sure that there is a cap sitting firmly on top of it rather than waving about in the air on the end of its cable. If you can't find the sparkplug, see if you can spot a hole where one used to be, and then walk back and look for it.

Remember it is illegal to drive motorised bikes through towns between the hours of 13.00 and 17.00 or indeed to make any loud noise.

Car hire

Only Syros and Andros have vehicles for rent at the moment. Details from the tourist offices.

NINE

Customs
and things you should know

Worry beads

Most Greek men have at least one set of worry beads which they produce at moments of tension, boredom or relaxation. These can be made of metal, plastic or wood and do not, as might be suspected derive from the rosary (in fact some scholars say that the rosary derives from them . . .) Some men are very adept at making the beads fly up and down their fingers and techniques vary. You will not see women using worry beads.

Drinking

As mentioned in Chapter Five, each refilled glass should be chinked with those of your companions. There are a variety of salutations used and as these can be rather confusing, just repeat whatever your host says.

Gestures — and avoiding trouble

One gesture that can be very confusing is the one used to indicate a negative reply to a question. The head is tipped sharply back and may be accompanied by a clicking noise made with the tongue. This gesture can be modified until only an eyebrow is moved almost imperceptibly and it takes a while to get used to it — you tend to think that either they haven't heard the question at all or are asking you to repeat or explain it.

The Greeks have a hand gesture that is far worse than our reversed victory sign in its meaning. To hold up your hand at eye level with fingers spread and palm outwards at someone is the worst

55

Serifos. The monastery at Kallitsos has a grand view as it sits imposingly at the top of a hillside approached only by a very uninviting road.

Syros. Vrontado. The Church of the Anastasis with its domed roof, on the inside of which has been painted a magnificent fresco.

possible insult and virtually a challenge to a duel. Even worse is to use two hands! I couldn't understand the look of horror on someone's face when I tried to use sign language to convey that I would be back in ten minutes by pointing to my watch and then holding up the appropriate number of fingers!

The word *malláka* is used frequently in conversation by Greek males and is the derogatory name for someone who satisfies their own physical desires. This is always used light-heartedly (there are far worse for when they are serious) but it is never acceptable for foreigners to use this word no matter how close you are or how long you have known somebody.

The evil eye

The Greek people believe strongly in the power of the evil eye — which is thought to be put on anyone who causes another to be envious of them. The way to avoid it is to wear one of the blue eye beads you will see in souvenir shops; or, if you think you might be about to get it, spit or make a noise similar to that of spitting. It can be a little disconcerting when, after you have admired someone's baby, they promptly expectorate.

The test to see if you have it is to try and recite at speed a piece of religious text, such as The Lord's Prayer. If you can't complete it or get muddled then you have got the evil eye and must go to one of the ladies who sit outside larger churches and she will remove it for you.

Religion

The Greek Orthodox faith is predominant everywhere in Greece although some islands have a proportion of Catholics. Orthodoxism is a splinter of the Catholic religion and has no connection with the Pope.

Services have a very relaxed atmosphere and no hymns or prayers are sung by the congregation. The faith seems to be strong and not as restrictive as some other forms of Christianity. Priests up to a certain "rank" are allowed to be married.

Churches and name days

The islands have literally hundreds of churches ranging from the very grand to those no bigger than the average garden shed! Every family tries to build a church at some time, often painting the roof sky blue to bring them nearer to God. Each church is named after a saint and in the smaller ones services are held only on the corresponding saint's day, once a year.

In the monasteries and larger churches, the whole village will attend services giving a festival atmosphere. Similarly all Greek people are named after saints and while birthdays are not celebrated, name days are marked by visiting with gifts the homes of fellow celebrants. There is little variety of names and so on the designated day for the most common names, such as Yannis and Kostas, restaurants and nightspots are well attended to the point of bursting!

Easter

Easter is a good time to visit Greece as the celebrations are as enthusiastic as Christmas is in England (Christmas is a lesser festival in Greece). Good Friday is a day of mourning. On the Saturday everyone goes to church for a midnight service after which there may be a firework display and each household lights a candle and tries to carry it home still lit. If successful, this is a sign of good luck for the next year.

On Easter Sunday, the traditional meal is of roast lamb, and wine is free in restaurants and *tavernas* if you can find one open. People carry red eggs and the usual "good morning" or "good evening" is replaced by "Christ is risen" to which the reply is "truly risen".

Transport to and within Greece is generally full at this time, so if you are planning an Easter trip book well in advance.

TEN

Language and alphabet

The main reason for including this chapter is that the effort of learning a few words of the language will be repaid many times by the reception you will get from the Greek people. Just to wish an islander "good morning" in his language is like paying him a compliment and although he may then assume that you speak fluent Greek and proceed to rattle on at top speed, you will be instantly accepted and liable to some of the very generous Greek hospitality.

Some of the smaller islands have very few English-speaking inhabitants and so a few of the most commonly used expressions may be helpful but a phrase book is a worthwhile investment and this chapter does not aim to replace them.

All Greek words in this book are spelt phonetically and not in the accepted English equivalent spelling. The syllable stress is very important in Greek and to put it in the wrong place can change the meaning completely. The accent denotes the syllable to be stressed.

The alphabet

The Greek alphabet is confusing because some of the letters that look like ours have a totally different sound:

A α	alpha	apple	Ξ ξ	ksee	rocks
B β	veta	never	O o	omikron	on
Γ γ	gamma	yellow or gap	Π π	pee	paper
Δ δ	thelta	then	P ρ	roe	roe
E ε	epsillon	enter	Σ σ	sigma	sand
Z ζ	zita	zip	T τ	taff	tiff

59

H η ita	cheese	Y υ ipsilon	police
Θ θ thita	thong	Φ φ fee	fend
I ι iota	pick	X χ hee	loch
K κ kappa	kind	Ψ ψ psee	synapse
Λ λ lamda	link	Ω ω omega	on (or owe
M μ mee	mother		at the end
N ν nee	nice		of words)

There are numerous letter combinations that make unpredictable sounds but this is rather off-putting for the beginner and so if you think you are ready for them, it is time to buy a teach yourself book.

Some conversational gambits

Meanwhile, it is useful to be able to form a few elementary questions and make one or two simple statements. Apart from ensuring your basic survival and comfort when there is no one around who speaks English this will, as said before, create a really friendly rapport with the local people.

The following lists will help you to put a few simple sentences together. Of course, these will not be in grammatically perfect Greek (a language cannot be learned so easily) but if you say them carefully they should be comprehensible to any Greek person, who will be absolutely delighted by the effort you have made. Remember to stress the accented syllables.

List A — basic statements and phrases

Yes: *neh*
No: *óhee*
Please/you are welcome: *parra kallóh*
Thank you: *efharistóe*
Good morning: *kallee máira*
Good evening: *kallee spáira*
Good night: *kallee níhta*
Hello/goodbye: *Yássoo* (*yássas* is more formal)
Greetings: *hyéretay*
Where is: *poo eénay*

I want: *thélloh*
I am: *éemay*
You are: *éesthay*
He/she is/there is/they are: *eenay*
We are: *ee már stay*
I have: *éhoe*
You have: *éhetay*
He/she/it has: *éhee*
We have: *éhoomay*
They have: *éhoon*
I don't want: *then thélloh*

60

Now if you turn to lists B, C and D you can add words to some of these to articulate your needs or ideas. Statements can be turned into questions by putting an intonation in your voice — to change "you are" to "are you", for instance.

List B — accommodation

hotel: *ksennoe doheé oh*
room: *thomátteeoh*
house: *spéetee*
bathroom: *bányoh*
shower: *dóos*

bed: *krevártee*
hot: *zéstee*
cold: *kréeoh*
blanket: *koo vérta*

List C — getting about

far: *makree áre*
near: *kondá*
bus: *leo fór eeoh*
taxi: *taxí*
ferry boat: *férry bott*
street: *óh thos*
road: *dróh moss*
corner: *go neár*
left: *arist erráh*

right: *thex ee áh*
single: *applóh*
return: *epist rofée*
ticket: *ee sit ée ree ah*
post office: *tahee droh mée oh*
laundry: *plind éereeoh*
bank: *tráp ezza*
telephone: *telléfonoh*
petrol: *vrin zée nee*

List D — eating and drinking

restaurant: *eest ee at ór ee oh*
food: *figh eet óh*
coffee: *kaféh*
tea: *ts ígh*
breakfast: *proh ee nóh*
sugar: *záh harree*

salt: *a lár tee*
pepper: *pip áir ee*
wine: *krass ée*
beer: *béerah*
water: *nair óh*
without: *hórris*
oil: *lárthee*

List E — other useful phrases and words

As you gain a little confidence — and begin to understand the replies you get — you will probably be able to make use of the following phrases and words — when shopping, for instance. Note that, although days and numbers have been given here, it is more difficult to talk about time, such as the hours of boats and buses, so that is when you ask for it to be written down!

How much is it?: *possóh kárnee eénay*
I want this: *thélloh aftóh*
I don't want this: *then thélloh aftóh*
What time does it leave?: *tee óra févyee*

What time does it arrive?: *tee óra ftáhnee*
Please write it down: *egráp settay parra kallóh*
Excuse me/sorry: *sig nóh mee*
I am an Englishman/woman: *éemay ángloss/angléeda*
Please speak slowly: *méelet ay argár parra kallóh*
Don't!: *mee!*
Go away!: *féev yet ay!*
Help!: *voh ée thee ah!*

Monday: *théftera*
Tuesday: *tréetee*
Wednesday: *tetártee*
Thursday: *pémptee*
Friday: *parraskevée*
Saturday: *sávatoh*
Sunday: *kirree akée*
one: *énna*
two: *thé oh*
three: *trée ya*
four: *téssera*
five: *pénday*
six: *éxee*
seven: *eptá*
eight: *oktoé*
nine: *enay yáh*
ten: *théka*
eleven: *én theka*

twelve: *thó theka*
twenty: *ée cosee*
thirty: *tree ánda*
forty: *sarránda*
fifty: *pen nínda*
sixty: *ex índa*
seventy: *ev tho mínda*
eighty: *ovthónda*
ninety: *en en índa*
one hundred: *eka tón*
two hundred: *thee ak ówsee ah*
three hundred: *track ówsee ah*
four hundred: *tétrak owsee ah*
five hundred: *pént ak owsee ah*
seven hundred: *eptak ówsee ah*
eight hundred: *okt ak ówsee ah*
nine hundred: *enyak ówsee ah*
thousand: *hill eeyá*

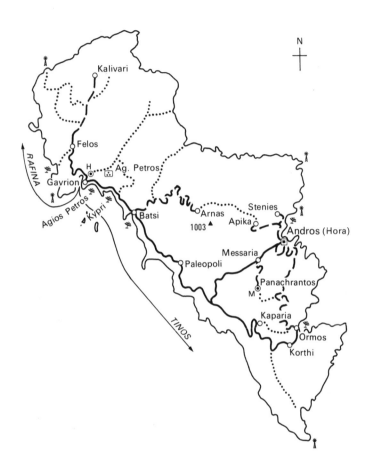

ANDROS

Scale 1:320 000

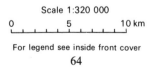

0   5   10 km

For legend see inside front cover

ELEVEN

Andros

Population: 14,000   Highest point: 1003 metres
Area: 405 sq. km.   Hotel beds: about 745

Andros is a much underestimated island and has even been described as "unquestionably uninteresting and dull" with which the author cannot agree. While Andros is not throbbing with life by either day or night, it has its own unique charms.

This is an exceptionally green and mountainous island where both sailors and ship owners have built grand houses on the mountainsides. The houses are well spaced in contrast to the typical clustering of most Greek towns and villages and at first glance seem to have no visible means of access. While the owners of these houses holiday on Andros, tourism is very new and limited to the small town of Batsi. On the north-west coast is the village of Gavrion with its deep water harbour where all the ferries dock.

The island's capital is Andros town or Hora on the east coast which is little visited by foreigners and so has none of the usual souvenir shops or "English spoken" signs.

The countryside is a network of stone walls constructed of piles of small stones alternating with large upended slabs that reflect the sunlight and when seen from the sea look like rows of primitive gravestones.

Arrival by sea

From Gavrion there are daily boats to Rafina three hours away and Tinos two hours away. Tickets can be purchased in Gavrion, Batsi or Hora but in Gavrion the office may only be open shortly before a boat is due in.

Buses from Hora via Batsi meet every boat and then make the

Andros. The smiling figure of the memorial to the Unknown Sailor waves cheerfully out to sea and the ruins of an ancient fortress. He is turning rather green but I trust this is due to age rather than sea-sickness!

return journey. If for any reason the bus is delayed the boats will wait for a reasonable length of time until it arrives.

The port police will confirm departure times and are very helpful. Their office is the grey building on the corner of the *paralia* (waterfront road) and the "uphill road" in Gavrion. Tel. 22250.

Road system

The road that links Gavrion, Batsi and Hora has a good surface and poses few problems except when leaving Batsi and Hora where it becomes steep and winding. From Gavrion to the northern villages, someone has had the bright idea of scattering fine gravel on top of the concrete road which gives about as much road holding as would petroleum jelly! The *paralia* in Gavrion resembles a lunar landscape with a myriad of potholes.

Buses The buses are all painted a light blue and cream on the outside which is where the uniformity ends as the drivers seem to compete to display the most brightly coloured plastic flowers and mascots. One enthusiastic driver has incorporated multicoloured interior lights which must be rather like taking a ride in a disco, after dark! Payment is made to the conductor during the journey, entry and exit from either door. The fare from Gavrion to Hora is 120 drachmas.

Taxis The standard island design is metallic grey paintwork with a sign on the top of the vehicle. All have meters.

Vehicle rental It is possible to hire cars and mopeds in Batsi. Tel. 41418.

Petrol Service stations are at Gavrion, Batsi and Hora, the latter can supply fuel for yachts. All are on the only road leaving each town and are easily spotted, with the exception of the one in Gavrion which is tucked away on the far right of the *paralia*.

Gavrion

Gavrion is the port of Andros and is mostly used as a terminus for visitors on their way to Batsi or Hora. By no means picturesque, this small town has bars, *tavernas* and a nearby disco among its shops and houses.

The *paralia* is the main road (all directions given with back to the sea, facing uphill) with a narrow road joining it at right angles on its right hand side that leads out of town.

Accommodation in Gavrion

Hotels There are five hotels in Gavrion:
— Afrodite (B), tel: 71209; 50 beds.
— Gavrion Beach (C), tel: 71312; 41 beds.
— Galaxy (D), tel: 71253; 44 beds.
— Athinaikon (E), tel: 71234; 20 beds.
— Aktaeon (E), tel: 71246; 20 beds.

Hotel Afrodite is described as a B class but apart from the decor of the reception area and the fact that the rooms have telephones, there is little to distinguish it from a C class. The owner's father, "Barbaryeorgos", was head chef to King Constantine and so the restaurant is definitely worth a visit. English spoken. It's situated 100m up on the left hand side of the "uphill" road with an inconspicuous and sharply gradiented driveway.

This family are constructing another B class hotel a little farther uphill and to the right. Not yet named, it should be ready by the time this book is published and will have, among its facilities, a swimming pool.

The Hotel Galaxy was previously named Kokkini; it has cheerful rooms, many of which have a sea view. All have bathrooms. It's opposite the jetty on the *paralia,* entrance next to the large glass-fronted cafe.

Rooms Rather spartan but clean rooms are available by enquiry at the haberdashery shop on the *paralia*. The rooms themselves are just behind this block. There is a communal bathroom.

Apartments Fully equipped bungalows with a sea view can be rented in Gavrion, tel: 71249.

Camping Deceptively called "Camping Andros", this camping ground is situated 300 metres from the port of Gavrion on the left hand side of the uphill road. Facilities advertised are:- hot water, electricity, mini-market, restaurant, snack bar, caravan and tent rental. When I visited, there was nothing except a field, which is exactly what is shown in the photograph on the advertisement. Tel. Athens 822549.

Eating out in Gavrion

There are five restaurants and tavernas in Gavrion. Of the restaurants, the one in the Hotel Afrodite and Three Star Restaurant are well worth trying. The latter has a good selection and is reasonably priced. It's the second building up from the *paralia* on the right hand side of the uphill road.

Of the *tavernas,* Yiannis' on the far left of the *paralia* is one of the best. There is not much to choose between the two *cafenions* on the *paralia,* both of which serve as waiting areas for would-be ferry passengers. The older, gloomy looking one sells local yoghurt and the newer glass fronted one has gooier cakes, and you can pass the time trying to remember not to hit your head on the lamp shades when you get up!

Nightlife in Gavrion
Disco Marabout Pronounced with a silent "t", this disco is 15 minutes walk from the port but a clearly marked minibus leaves from the *paralia* when required and returns at 02.00 hrs. on Thursdays and Saturdays, no charge is made. The bus also visits Batsi and Hora but no regular times have been arranged (tel. 71391). Situated just off the road opposite Ag. Petros beach, the disco has a café, pizzeria and *taverna.* In the winter, the disco becomes a weekend *bazouki.*
Idrousa Bar This cosily decorated establishment describes itself as a café/bar but has the appearance and atmosphere of a bar. The selection of music is excellent and Takis is a very friendly host. English spoken. On colder evenings sitting close to the fireplace while making a fuss of one of their two enormous cats is recommended.

Useful addresses in Gavrion
Police Their building is hidden up a pathway from the far left of the *paralia* where it masquerades as a house, and is only given away by the Greek flag flying outside. Tel: 71220.
Post Office First turning right on the uphill road (ten metres).
Telephone Office On the left of the path leading up from the side of the port police office (five metres).
Banks Gavrion is served by mobile banks in summer. If you get desperate for cash, ask the people at the Afrodite Hotel to arrange for it to call or take a bus to Hora.
Reading matter It is not possible to buy either books or newspapers in any other language than Greek. There are two maps of the island both in poster form. The one with a concise history in English on the back is the better map, the other one has nothing on the reverse side.

Batsi

This pretty little town covers a hillside and bay of a small cove eight kilometres from Gavrion. The usual tourist facilities have

Andros. Batsi. The island's resort town has lost none of it's charm in its recent development and has some excellent beaches.

appeared here over the last few years and it seems to have been decided that this should be the main resort — which visitors are happy to go along with as Batsi has some fine beaches.

The town is approached by a narrow winding road that having led down the hillside to the north of the town, passes between the hotels and the beach before reaching the small harbour with its shops and cafés. The road leaves by way of the main hill which it ascends sharply before proceeding on to Hora.

Accommodation in Batsi

Hotels All the hotels in Batsi are along the *paralia* and, as the names are in large lettering, are not difficult to find.
— Lykion (B), tel: 41214; 28 beds.
— Chryssi Akti (C), tel: 41236; 118 beds.
— Skouna (C), tel: 41315; 38 beds.
— Avra (D), tel: 41216; 24 beds.
— Krinos (D), tel: 41232; 21 beds.
Apartments Fully furnished apartments are for rent in Villa Volika. Tel: 41498. All have hot water, balcony and private bathroom.
Rooms People with rooms to let meet the buses from Gavrion in the summer. The residential area of Batsi is at the top of, and behind, the hill.

Where to eat in Batsi

Most of the eating places are halfway up the hill opposite the little jetty. Try Yiannis restaurant and Stamatis Taverna. There are *cafenions* along the *paralia* near the shops and two more *tavernas*.

Night life

Chaf Disco Crowning the hill on the approach road from Gavrion, it has a good view of the harbour and town.
Blue Sky Disco Near the Chrissi Akti Hotel on the back road.

Useful addresses in Batsi

Police Follow the signposts for the O.T.E. from the left hand side of Hotel Avra. When you reach it, continue along the same street until it branches left. Look for the flag. Tel. 4202.
Telephone office Well signposted from the *paralia,* the office is five minutes trudge uphill on the right hand side. This O.T.E. doubles as an ironmongers and two of its three cubicles closely resemble cupboards! Unfortunately it is difficult to get through on overseas calls, and this, coupled with the fact that the proprietor does sheet metalwork that involves hammering out stubborn areas,

means that you need to allow extra time and cash for your calls!
Buses and taxis The bus stop and taxi rank are both on the *paralia* near Hotel Avra. Bus times from the information office opposite the hotel.

Banks There is a National Bank of Greece office, slightly larger than the average telephone kiosk, on the right hand corner of the Hotel Avra block. Mobile banks visit from Hora.

Andros town: Hora

This unremarkable town can be rather unfriendly to tourists and apart from stocking a Greek-produced English language newspaper makes no provision for them. Hora is built around one long street that is reported to have once been a ravine. A paved square sits between this pedestrian only street and a small clinic behind which are the bus station and taxi rank.

In the downhill direction, the street houses the Post Office, O.T.E., four banks, two museums, Hotel Egli, cinema and numerous shops. If you follow this street to the sea, you come to the weather beaten statue of The Unknown Sailor who waves grotesquely out to sea and to the ruined fortress of Kato Kastro.

To the south is an attractive looking beach that is unfortunately very exposed to the winds that almost constantly buffet this coast. To the north is the harbour area and the air-conditioned Disco Remedzo.

The bus station has a completely unintelligible timetable, even if you read and understand Greek, but the drivers will point you to the appropriate bus if you say where you want to go. As well as back to Batsi or Gavrion, buses go to Stenies, Arni and Korthion. O Stathmos Restaurant is the nearest thing to a waiting room and has excellent food. The best eating places seem to be out of town and worth a visit are the *tavernas* at Menites, Katafelos and Katakilos.

Hotels in Hora are:
— Xenia (B), tel: 22270; 42 beds.
— Paradisos (B), tel: 22187; 76 beds.
— Egli (C) tel: 22303; 30 beds.

Useful telephone numbers for Hora are: Police — 22300; Clinic — 22758; Agricultural Bank — 22368; National Bank — 22232; Ionic and Popular — 22291.

Nets!

What to see and do on Andros

There are not a great number of sights to see on Andros so they have been assembled here rather than under separate town headings according to location.

Agios Petros Tower This unusual piece of craftsmanship and architecture is situated four kilometres from Gavrion along the road that leaves from the far left of the *paralia;* the last kilometre is unmade. Constructed from interlocking stones without the use of mortar, the tower stands four metres high and has a circumference of 21 metres. There is much controversy as to its function as it is too far from the sea to have been a lighthouse or signal tower and is too small to have been any sort of fortification. The age of the tower is also in dispute and varies from the Pelasgian to the Byzantine era.

Monastery of Panachrantos (1158 A.D.) If you can bear the thought of a two-hour donkey ride each way with little to see at the end of it, visit this monastery. The journey starts from Messaria near Hora.

Museum of modern art This small museum is well signposted from the bus station in Hora from where it is a five minute walk. Entrance is free and the collection is well worth seeing as the variety of exhibits ensures that there must be something for everyone's taste. To my mind, the *pièce de resistance* is moving, musical sculpture in the basement. Open from 10.00 to 13.00 and 17.00 to 20.00 hrs. Monday to Saturday, closed Tuesdays. Free admission.

Archaeological museum On the main street in Hora, on the corner to the left of the archway near the bookstore, facing downhill and conspicuous by its brown tiled steps. This very sophisticated and modern building has remote control television cameras to watch visitors as they view the displays. Labelling is in English and has been thoughtfully done to give a history of Andros from ancient times to the present day. The prize exhibit is the Hermes of Andros, a splendid marble statue of the God Hermes that has only recently been returned to the island from Athens to commemorate the opening of the museum.

An English language video is shown on request but is disappointing in that it deals with Greek history in general rather than that relating to Andros, and is neither well made nor a good quality recording. Admission 50 drachmas, 30 drachmas for students. Open 9.00 to 15.30 hrs. Monday to Saturday, closed Tuesdays.

Beaches

The island's best beaches are at Batsi where two long sandy stretches are popular destinations in summer. Agios Petros near the Marabout Disco and Kypri beach in front of Hotel Perrakis, 1½ km and 3 km respectively south from Gavrion, also have attractive beaches with safe swimming, while the beach at Gavrion is somewhat less inviting.

The coast between Batsi and Korthion has many sandy coves visible from the bus but most of these are completely inaccessible by land. A boat from Batsi does trips to smaller beaches between Batsi and Gavrion.

Historical background

Like most of the Cyclades islands, Andros is thought to have been first colonised by the Kares and in 1000 B.C. by the Ionians.

When Themostokles came to Andros to collect the Athenian tribute after the victory at Salamis, the islanders refused to pay, which led to an attack which the Andrians thwarted. Despite the islanders' subsequent help to the Athenians at Plataea, they were not forgiven and the island was divided between Athenian colonists who levied high taxes on the locals. As a result, the Andrians changed sides and supported Sparta in the Peloponnesian war. The new Spartan governors were no less stringent than the Athenians had been and life did not improve until the island came under control of Byzantium. In the meantime, the island unsuccessfully resisted an attack by Rome and consequently all the islanders were exiled to Boetia. On their subsequent return, the island was a shell of its former wealth and many homes had been looted.

After the Venetian occupation, the Turks captured the island in 1566 but left the inhabitants much to their own devices. The Turks were ousted in the War of Independence and life was comparatively peaceful until the Second World War, when the island was heavily bombed — though happily no evidence of this remains.

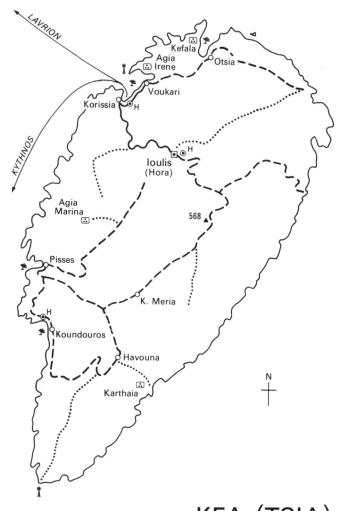

KEA (TSIA)

Scale 1:150 000

0   5 km

For legend see inside front cover

TWELVE

Kea

Population: 3,000   Highest point: 568 metres
Area: 121 sq. km.   Hotel beds: 286

Kea, also known as Tsia, although close to the Greek mainland, has only recently started to have foreign visitors. Athenian shipowners have built some grand houses on the island including one next to the port of Korissia in the style of an old English rectory, looking strangely out of place near some palm trees and a typically Greek church.

The island is fairly mountainous and the communities are scattered to all points of its rocky terrain. An unusual number of trees grow on Kea including many oak trees on the higher ground, while those nearer the valleys have a delicate pink blossom in early spring and look vulnerable against the barren background. A large number of oak trees are covered in a strange looking furry green lichen which appears to be damaging the trees.

The most visited towns are Otsia and Voukari north of the port, and Pisses and Koundouros on the west coast. Unlike most of the Cyclades, the main town does not bear the same name as the island itself but is shown on maps as Ioulis. However, it is more commonly referred to by the locals as Hora. Ioulis is on high ground and straddles a slight dip in between two hills. When seen from above, the town's two largest churches Agios Dimitris and Agios Spiridon stand out in their beige and red colour scheme in contrast to the small white houses.

The people of Kea are unusually friendly and helpful.

Arrival by sea

Kea is linked to Lavrion (two hours) on the mainland and the island

77

of Kythos (1½ hours) by a small ferry, "The Kastriani Kea" — but this ship will be replaced for servicing shortly and a much larger vessel may replace it. The current ship can carry 6-8 vehicles. Only snacks are available. Tickets can be purchased at Lavrion, Kythnos or at the bank/shop (see Useful addresses) in Hora or any of the ticket offices in the port of Korissia. Tickets can also be bought on the boat but the staff get rather irritated and it will cost 25% more on board!

There are daily sailings in each direction in summer, falling to five per week in winter. It is possible to change at Kythnos for Piraeus but obviously more expensive and time-consuming.

The port police building is attached to the flag pole that leans over the jetty.

Road system

The roads on Kea are not good as the surrounding hillsides have not been as extensively terraced as on other islands and there are frequent landslides which deposit boulders, trees and soil on the roads. The steep road between Korissia and Hora is potholed tarmac but the remaining roads are unsurfaced which makes them impassable in winter. There are plans to improve the standard but like everything else in Greece, it will take a long time.

Petrol This can be bought only in Korissia. The old fashioned pumps are 300 metres along the road to Hora.

Buses The two buses are both blue and cream. The newer of the two has curtains that refuse to stay open so you have to hold them if you want to see where you are going. This vehicle does the run from Hora to Otsia via Korissia before and after every boat arrival and to fit in with the schoolchildren's hours. This means there are journeys approximately every two hours in summer and two per day in winter.

The older vehicle does the hour long journey from Hora to Havouna in the south, via Kato Meria. This service mainly carries the schoolchildren and weekly shoppers who are brought from the isolated villages. There are four buses per day in summer and two in winter. On Sundays there is a bus to Pisses from Korissia.

Details of bus times are displayed in the window of the second travel office from the jetty in Korissia. These must be taken as a guide only, as they vary according to what time the children get out of school, whether the driver wants to get home early or whether he is going to drop off a friend who lives off the usual route!

Every boat is met by a bus to Hora via Otsia so if you are told there isn't one, find the bus driver and tell him the policeman assured you one was due. The driver lives near Voukari and so is reluctant to do the trip if there are only a few tourist passengers as it means he gets home later!

Buses leave from outside the garage near the jetty in Korissia and from the only level piece of ground in Hora (you will see what this means)! If you miss the Hora bus as it leaves the jetty, remember it first goes to Otsia in the north before returning via Korissia to Hora so you can catch it by waiting at the junction of the two roads (provided the driver hasn't gone home)!

Taxis Taxis also wait for the boats having brought a full load down from Hora. If you can't see one at other times, ask in the supermarket on the *paralia* in Korissia or in the souvenir shop near the post office in Hora. These people will be willing to telephone if you ask nicely and pay for the call, and they have the knack of knowing were the drivers might be having an ouzo or playing cards.

Maps The newsagent in Korissia and the souvenir shop in Hora sell an adequate map of the island with some interesting grammar in its information on the reverse. There is a small booklet about the island in English that might help you decide from the photographs where you want to go.

Accommodation on Kea

Hotels There are only four hotels on the island so all accommodation will be included here.

— Hotel I. Isia Mas (B), tel: 31305. A new white building behind the beach that is identifiable even though it doesn't display a name sign.

— Ioulis (B), tel: 22177. This hotel has a spectacular view due to its position on the very top of the left hand hill in Hora as you approach from the port, which also means you have got a spectacular climb to get to it! Where the road ends and the street begins in Hora is an archway, through which can be seen a sign for the hotel. Unfortunately this is the only one. Follow the arrow to the left as it climbs up and eventually past some doorways on the left. Just past here is a precarious flight of steps on the left which can be easily overlooked. Unless you are on your own, it might be a good idea to leave someone at the bottom of these steps with the luggage while someone else, preferably the fittest, goes up to see if there is a room available. The path turns left at the summit and becomes a covered passageway under the old castle. The word Kastro has been painted on the concrete path. Turn right and there it is. Maybe it isn't all that far (150 metres) but when you finally get to the top, particularly if you have smoker's lungs and heavy bags, only to find it full, it seems like Everest.

— Kea Beach Hotel (B), tel: 22144. This 150 bed hotel is one of the few buildings at Koundouros. They run a minibus to Hora and Korissia that meets each boat as there is only one public transport bus per week.

— Hotel Karthea (C), tel: 31222. This is the very "un-Greek islandish" building on the corner of the *paralia* and the Hora road. It has comfortable rooms with private bathrooms for which they are reluctant to heat hot water if there aren't many guests.

Rooms Korissia has new houses behind the beach that have been built for summer room rental. In Hora there is a guest house Filoxenia (B) that has five attractively decorated bedrooms with separate bathroom. The owner doesn't sympathise with people who like to wash daily in hot water and will wring every drachma out of you that he can get. Follow that main road uphill past the butcher's shops and up the steps that start between the restaurant and the supermarkets. When you get up as far as a cake shop on the left and a shoe shop on the right, the cardboard name sign is on the right hand side of the shoe shop frontage.

Apartments Manos apartments in Koundouros advertise on the *paralia* in Korissia. Tel: 2224.

Camping There are no camping sites on Kea at the moment so when the hotel rooms are full, camping is tolerated on all but main town beaches — but of course there are no facilities.

Food

There is no great variety of places to eat on Kea but the standard is high. The large glass-fronted restaurant on the harbour in Korissia has excellent food but it is served rather cold even by Greek standards.

In Hora, there are two tavernas, one restaurant and a pizza bar. The taverna nearest the arch by the bus stop is small and has a friendly atmosphere. The food is good but choice is limited. On the corner of the main street opposite the supermarkets is the restaurant where live Greek music is often played in the evening.

Ioulis. This small friendly family taverna has some unusual dishes cooked to a high standard.

The Kastriani Kea. One of the smaller car ferries that serve Kea and Kythnos from Lavrion. The arrival in winter is a great event for the local people who all turn out to see the comings and goings.

The food is good and inexpensive.

The pizza bar has a way of running out of just what you happen to fancy at the time and the service is so slow that you wait fifteen minutes for a coffee when there is no one else in there. It's opposite the bus stop in Hora.

On the right going uphill on the main street is the café which occupies half of what is otherwise the mayor's office, a detached brightly painted house. Usually full of old timers playing cards, this cafe has the distinction of serving the cheapest cup of coffee of any of the six islands.

The cake shop is on the left hand side of the main street — see directions for Filoxenia guest house. They have a good selection of gateaux but surprisingly no yoghurt.

Night life

The island has three discotheques as well as live Greek music in the restaurant in Hora.

Medusa Disco On the *paralia* at Voukari.

Kea Disco About 500 metres out of Korissia along the road to Hora on the left hand side, it is the first building after the garage. Down some steps from the road, this disco consists of a wooden floor in the middle of a field behind which is a paddock occupied by two cows. One wonders what the late night music does to the milk yield!

Kea Beach Disco At the Kea Beach Hotel; minibuses leave from Korissia and Hora to take people out to the disco. No organised schedule. Tel: 22144.

Useful addresses for Kea

Police The police station in Korissia between the Hotel Karthea and the restaurant. Tel. 31300.

Telephone office Half way up the main street in Hora on the right hand side.

Post office To the left of the bus stop facing the archway in Hora.

Banks There is no bank as such on Kea but there is an agent who changes travellers cheques or Eurocheques. In the supermarket opposite the restaurant on Hora, look for the No.1 cigarette advertisement above the door. At the top of the main street next to a clothes store.

Doctor From the bus stop in Hora where there is also a pharmacy, the doctor's office is signposted with a red cross.

Reading matter The newsagent in Korissia keeps English newspapers in summer with a small selection of English books. Kea Beach Hotel has books for sale but no facilities for borrowing or exchanging exist.

Centres of population

Korissia

The port of Kea is still attractive despite the hideous hotel and glass fronted restaurants. The crisp white church sits on a promontory of rock at the mouth of the bay. The most noticeable building however is the solitary house opposite the harbour that looks as if it has been transported from the grounds of an English rectory. The greenery that separates it from the sea is such a vivid colour it is almost fluorescent. Between the jetty and the church is a sandy beach backed by two hotels and new houses with rooms for rent. The restaurant, café and shops are all side by side along the harbour. Just outside the town is a derelict factory with its tall chimney still standing like a memorial to the lost industry.

Hora: Ioulis

This is a charming town that forms a white arc in a depression between two hills, five kilometres from Korissia. Although some drivers are willing to navigate the narrow archway and drive into the main street, most vehicles park on the small area of level ground at the top of the winding road from the port. Through the archway the main street goes left and eventually up to the hotel on the top of the smaller of the two hills, while to the right it goes past all the major shops, eating places and offices before curving left from whereon it is stepped. By picking your way through the ever narrowing street, inevitably encountering deadends that lead only to someone's turquoise back door guarded by flaming geraniums, you eventually come to the top of the hill and are rewarded by an amazing view of the town, surrounding hills, sea and even the mainland on a clear day.

Voukari and Otsia

Approximately three and six kilometres from Korissia respectively, these two villages are pleasant places to stay and while as yet there are no hotels, they both have places to eat and are tourist orientated. Voukari has a disco and a larger selection of *tavernas* and souvenir shops while Otsia has more rooms to rent. Both have good beaches.

Pisses and Koundouros

Koundouros has the oversized Kea Beach Hotel and this is the centre of most of the facilities there. The shop, discotheque and bar are open to non-residents.

Pisses has the island's best beach and it is therefore surprising that these two towns are inadequately served by the public bus.

What to see and do on Kea

Museum From all accounts, the museum in Hora is worth visiting. It was closed for redecoration during my visit and I couldn't persuade them to let me in. It's the large building with barred windows downhill from the telephone office on the right hand side of the main street. Opening hours yet to be decided.

Agia Irene Most of the exhibits in Hora have come from Agia Irene where archaeologists have excavated ruins of a Minoan palace, temple and road. The site is surrounded by a wire fence and the public are not admitted but it is possible to see quite well from the boundary. Some of the ruins are below the watermark 500 metres from Voukari towards Otsia next to the little church on the rocky promontory.

Excursion Although there is nothing to do when you arrive there, it is worth taking the bus out to Kato Meria and Havouna if you want to see what the more remote parts of the island are like. The journey takes an hour in each direction and only waits a few minutes before turning round. Regular public bus from Hora, fare 240 drachmas return.

Agia Marina One kilometre from Pisses towards Korissia are the ruins of an ancient tower and monastery from the middle of which sprouts a comparatively modern church giving sharp contrast between the grey rocky ruins and the freshly whitewashed church. The weekly bus to Pisses will drop you off where the track leads from the main road unless you want to take a taxi (600 drachmas).

Beaches

As mentioned above, the island's best beach is at Pisses with

Koundouros a close second. Both have long quiet stretches of golden sand.

Korissia has a small beach but this is rather exposed in its proximity to the road. The beaches between Korissia and Voukari and those at Voukari and Otsia are also near the road but out of the port there is less traffic.

Historical background

At Ag. Irene have been excavated ruins of a Minoan colony but the evidence of a Neolithic settlement at Kephala indicates that the island was inhabited from 3000 B.C. Houses built by the Venetian aristocracy in their occupation in the thirteenth century can still be seen and descendents of the conquerors still lived on the island up to the time of the Turkish occupation. A noted rebel against the Turks, Lambros Katsonis, managed to escape a flotilla of Turkish ships when they thought they had him blockaded in port. By ordering his troops to take the ships across a narrow piece of land, he left the bewildered Turks safely behind.

Mythology had it that the god Minos fathered the Kean race. Aristeus, son of Apollo, taught the islanders agricultural skills including the growing of olives.

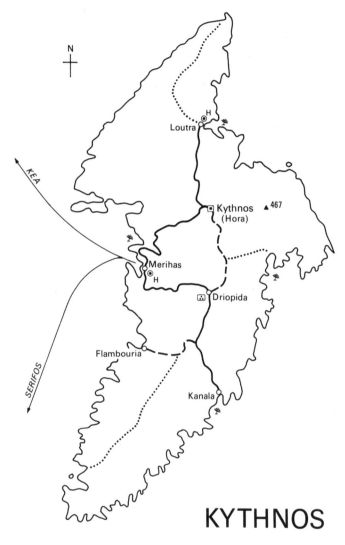

N

KEA

SERIFOS

H
Loutra

□ Kythnos
(Hora)

▲ 467

Merihas
H

⊡ Driopida

Flambouria

Kanala

KYTHNOS

Scale 1:150 000

0   5 km

THIRTEEN

Kythnos

Population: 2,000   Highest point: 467 metres
Area: 86 sq. km.   Hotel beds: 251

Another quiet island where tourism is a new but growing industry. The four towns are fairly evenly spaced along the length of the island while the east side is almost uninhabited. Even in its greenest season, Kythnos has a barren rocky appearance with its terraced hillsides and valleys strewn with ancient walls and primitive crumbling stone houses. In the area around the port of Merihas, some of the land has been cultivated and plots of fruit trees and vines are interspersed between the untended land where sheep and goats graze.

The island is reputed to have 63 beaches, the majority of which are inaccessible by road or even on foot without the aid of climbing gear. All have coarse sand of a greyish brown colour.

The island is not wealthy and in its capital Hora (Kythnos), the houses are of a mixture of building materials and little has been done to keep up their appearance. From above, the red tiled roofs resemble M. de Gallard's painting of a French village but from street level Hora looks like a Greek shanty town.

The second town of Driopida is more attractive and its maze of little streets provides an opportunity for seeing an unspoilt Greek mountain village.

The northernmost tip of the island has hot springs at Loutra where a small resort has risen, originally as a result of Greek visitors taking the cure for rheumatism and arthritis and now used by tourists drawn to the beach.

At the opposite tip of the island is the village of Kanala, which is being extended by rooms built for summer rental as this is the most picturesque spot on the island.

Arrival by sea

Kythnos is served by two separate boat services. The first uses a typical ferry which departs from Piraeus and, after the 3½ hour journey to Kythnos, goes on to Serifos, Sifnos and Milos before turning round. The second service uses smaller boats that can carry only a half-dozen vehicles to Lavrion on the mainland. The outward journey from Lavrion is via Kea and the total journey takes about five hours depending on how long loading takes there. While for both services it is possible to buy tickets on the boats, for the smaller boats the fare is at least 25% cheaper from on shore ticket offices, for some strange reason.

Road system

The roads are surprisingly good on Kythnos for a quiet island. All are tarmac and in reasonable repair.

Petrol There is a service station in Hora.

Buses The island has two buses, both blue and cream. In Merihas they wait at the bottom of the ramp that leads to the café and shops above the jetty. In the summer a regular service operates between Hora and Loutra, Merihas, Driopida and Kanala. Timetables are not posted but enquire at cafés or of the drivers to ascertain the departure times. Just look enquiringly as you go to get off and the driver will automatically say the times of the return journeys.

Taxis This is another "two taxi island". The older of the two vehicles takes ten passengers long distances with only slight suffocation and circulation impairment to the occupants.

Accommodation on Kythnos

Despite recent building, in July and August all accommodation quickly becomes full, at which time it is acceptable to camp on the beaches without hindrance from the police. but it is better to choose an out of town beach to run less risk of complaint from local residents, who can cause the police to move you on.

Hotels Merihas has two hotels, the Hotel Poseidon which boldly displays its name on a rather out of place tall building on the *paralia,* and the Xenia which is rather more reserved such that binoculars are required to read the name plate from the slope above the jetty where it is sited.

— Poseidon (Merihas), (C); tel: 31244; 158 beds.
— Xenia Anagenissis, (Loutra), (C), tel: 31217; 93 beds.
— Xenia (Merihas), a new hotel, now operative, but at the time of going to press official details are not yet available from EOT.

Rooms New buildings along the *paralia* display rooms for rent signs. If you have any difficulty locating a room, ask the port or regular policeman who meets the boat, or enquire at the Ionian Ticket Office half way along the sloping road above the jetty.

Camping There are no established camping grounds on Kythnos and not likely to be any in Merihas at least, as land is available only in small plots giving insufficient room for this type of project.

Food

There is little point in describing locations of various eating places as Merihas isn't big enough to cause difficulty in finding anything! During the author's (out of season) stay on the island, every eating place in Merihas was closed so the only pertinent comment is that the local supermarket sells brands of corned beef and biscuits on which it is possible to live without detriment to health!

Night life

There isn't a great choice of places to go in the evenings on Kythnos so all the possibilities are included here rather than under their town headings.

Kavas Disco This air-conditioned disco is on the sloping road above the jetty in Merihas.

Kythnos Disco Two hundred metres from Loutra on the road to Hora, this open air disco is set in the fields on the left hand side of the road.

In the *tavernas* in Driopida, the locals get together and dance to *bazouki* music played by their friends. You can join in or just watch — either way it is great entertainment.

What to see and do

Test the healing powers of the thermal spa at Loutra in the old hospital-like hotel there. Who knows, it might just be the cure for that creaky joint or bad back!

There are some unspectacular ruins at Katakefala and Driopida. The former are of an old castle and is known as the Oriastro Kastro. The latter are ruins of walls, houses and the fortress of Vryokastro.

Driopida is a lovely town to wander around for those of you with a good sense of direction.

Centres of population

Merihas
The port of Merihas spreads around a small inlet in the rocky hillside with the jetty at one end and the Hotel Poseidon at the other. In between are rooms to rent, *tavernas,* cafés, another hotel, supermarkets and souvenir shops, though Merihas would still only be described as a village.

Hora
This is an unattractive town that has very few shops, *tavernas* or *cafenions.* The bus stops at a small square from which the road closest to the children's playground leads to the main street and a larger square down some steps to the right. In this area are the telephone office, post office and police station. The doctor's surgery cum pharmacy is the building with the green door (until they redecorate!) at the top of the stairs up from the left of the main street facing uphill. The present occupant is an extremely helpful young man who says his English is rusty but he never has any difficulty with non-Greek-speaking patients. There is also a small bank here.

One of the occupants is a little old lady who must be a bit senile. If you start going down the steps to the square, she will ask you if you *really* are going down. This is rather disconcerting if you understand what she is saying, and confusing if you can't.

Driopida
This maze of narrow streets with steps leading off in all directions is a pleasant little town. There are more shops and *tavernas* here than in Hora. These are on the main street known as the Agora (market) that meanders through the town and joins the main square where the buses wait, via a large attractive church. One of the *taverna* owners is very enthusiastic about his knowledge of English and, if visitors are in short supply and trade is slack, will follow you in case you think of anything you need to ask him.

Loutra

Loutra is a strange little town. One of the first buildings you see is a very large grey hotel that looks exactly like a hospital — quite fitting considering the large number of elderly rheumatics and arthritics who used to visit to benefit from the thermal baths there. It is possible to pay to take the waters even if you are not staying there.

The remainder of the buildings are an odd mixture of the dilapidated original bath house and a new supermarket, *taverna* and houses.

Kanala

The most attractive of the towns on Kythnos, Kanala, has many new buildings that can only be rooms to rent. There is a splendid church set in a small shady wooded area that is also the setting for a *taverna*.

Beaches

The beach at Merihas is rather too close to the road and shops for comfort but over the first hill on the road to Hora is a more secluded spot. This beach, like most on Kythnos, is of a grey brown coarse sand, backed by the occasional tree. Other beaches are at Fikiado, Kolona, Lefkas and Episcope but perhaps the most attractive is at Kanala.

Historical background

Kythnos has little of historical or mythological interest. This is yet another island once inhabited by a large number of snakes and it got its name from its sixth-century king who succeeded the Minoans. It has been ruled by the Minoans, Driopes, Rhodians and the Cozzadini family that still survives today in Bologna.

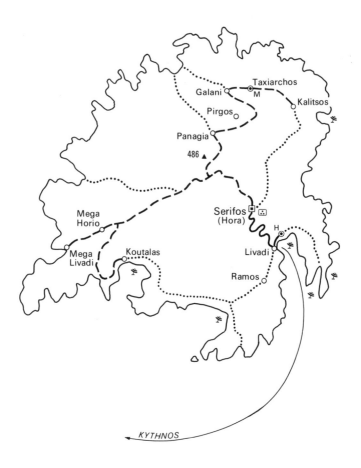

SERIFOS

Scale 1:125 000

0   5 km

For legend see inside front cover

FOURTEEN

Serifos

Population: 1,000   Highest point: 486 metres
Area: 75 sq. km.   Hotel beds: 139

Serifos is one of the least commercialised of the Cyclades islands; it is also one of the least populated with a winter figure of 500 residents.

The locals will tell you that there are eight towns other than the capital Serifos town or Hora. By our standards, Panagia, Galani, Kalitsos, Mega Horio, Mega Livadi, Koutalas and Ramos are small villages. The eighth, Livadi, is the port and has the only hotels of the island. Hence it is the centre for the small number of tourists.

The communities are invariably found on an impossibly steep hillside and houses are seldom built in the valleys or on low ground. The hillsides are carved up into terraces to prevent landslides and aid passage by donkey to the houses that are often sited a kilometre from the nearest dirt track and many more kilometres from the nearest village. The people of Serifos must have very solitary natures to have caused them to live so far away from other dwellings.

Most families keep goats, sheep and chickens with the occasional cow or pig. Although the terraces are covered with lush grass in the winter, little of the land is cultivated and only the wild narcissus are harvested and sent with the fish caught locally to Athens. In spite of the fact that few vines are in evidence, every family produces its own wine with varying degrees of resination and sweetness.

The only industry of the island is the mining at Mega Livadi where the excavation of ore has been replaced by digging for gravel as a building material. This is a light pink in colour and where it has been used as a road surface it looks very strange in contrast to the deep reddish brown of the rocks into which the road has

Serifos. Livadi. A parking lot for the island's most comfortable form of transport. The capital: Hora, is visible in the background.

been carved.

Arrival by sea

Ferries dock at Livadi, six kilometres away from Hora. Serifos is linked to Piraeus by a 5½ hour journey via Kythnos, and to Milos 2 hours away. There are two boats daily in summer, reduced to two per week in winter. The ferries used are large and carry goods, lorries and cars.

Tickets can be purchased in Livadi from the mini-market or from either of the travel offices behind the bakery.

The port police office is opposite the bakery and although no English is spoken, they are willing to help if you are willing to mime! Tel: 51470.

Road system

This heading should really appear in inverted commas as the word 'road' on Serifos is a euphemism.

Twenty metres from the jetty in Livadi, the concrete gives way to compacted sand that has been cunningly sculptured to trap as much water as possible after each rain. This provides an amusing pastime of picking your way through the puddles and taking running jumps over the streams. When the concrete reappears as the route to Hora, it also has great chunks worn out of it and even the best suspension can't cope with the bumps. Two kilometres outside Hora, the concrete and dirt road begins. The roads are wide and on the sharp bends, mirrors have been replaced to aid visibility. In places, the local gravel has been used as a surface, which gives better protection against the quagmires that develop after a heavy rain making passage completely impossible even by lorry. In winter, the buses and taxis will travel only between Hora and Livadi so if you don't have your own vehicle, you don't go to any of the other towns.

Buses The island has two buses, one turquoise and cream, the other grey. From the *paralia* in Livadi, the buses leave for Hora where they do a circuit of the island. In July and August, the service is theoretically hourly. In June and September there are four per day dwindling to one per day until the roads are bad enough to permit passage only between Livadi and Hora.

Taxis The two taxis are grey and easily distinguishable from other vehicles. When not waiting on the *paralia* or carrying passengers, the Livadi taxi can be contacted by telephoning 51245. The Hora taxi waits in the square, tel: 51435.

Petrol There are no service stations as we know them but petrol can be purchased from the hardware store opposite the public lavatories.

Accommodation

Hotels The island's four hotels are in Livadi.

— Perseus (B), tel: 51273; 20 beds. Along the *paralia,* midway between Serifos Beach and Maestrali.

— Serifos Beach Hotel (C), tel: 51468; 63 beds. This comfortable hotel is run by a friendly multilingual family. All rooms have private bathroom. It's a relatively tall building with a churchlike projection on top, bearing the word "Hotel", 200 metres from the jetty and signposted from the *paralia* behind Casa Dora self-service and rooms. One unusual feature is a mid afternoon chorus from hundreds of frogs in a neighbouring pool. They all seem to start at exactly the same instant and sound like hundreds of ducks except for the leader who makes a noise similar to that used to encourage horses! It only lasts for five minutes and so will not keep you awake at night!

— Maestrali (C), tel: 51381; 40 beds. This attractive building has no name board to advertise it but it is easily distinguishable by its three floors of arched front-facing balconies. It is 300 metres from the jetty along the *paralia*.

— Cyclades Hotel (E), no telephone; 16 beds. This one is on the back road next door to the travel office.

Guest House Up the dirt road that ascends from the jetty, a fifteen metres fairly steep climb, is a guest house.

Food

There are a half-dozen *tavernas* and restaurants along the *paralia* at Livadi. Try Sea Horse Restaurant and Lobster House Taverna. There is a "fast food" establishment on the back road behind the port police office.

Night life

Livadi has two discotheques. Scorpion is on the *paralia* near the
jetty and Hundred Pipers is on the back road towards Hora —
ten minutes walk from the kiosk. There is a Greek-owned bar
named Froggies Pub near to the Serifos Beach Hotel. The title must
derive from the biology of the neighbouring pond rather than the
nationality of its owner.

What to see and do

Boat trips There are organised boat trips from Livadi to some of
the island's other beaches. The price depends on the number of
passengers and can range from 200-500 drachmas. Be warned that
this is an unlicensed enterprise and if anything should go wrong,
there is no chance of compensation. The boats are small and can
only leave in very calm seas.

Monastery of Taxiarchos On the road from Galani to Kallitsos,
this is now the home of just one monk who visits Athens regularly.
Of course one of his visits coincided with the author's visit to Serifos
so it can only be reported that the monastery is reputed to have
many old and beautiful frescos. The red roof on the chapel looks
even more quaint with a sunset behind it.

Walking To go to Serifos you must have a desire to get away from
it all and an ability to climb hillsides. Walking is the only other
pastime and as all the walks must be across the terraced hillsides,
there are no ready-made routes to adhere to. Sensible shoes are
essential. From Livadi to Hora, the way has been interspersed with
steps as a short cut to the uphill meandering of the road. The
surface is very uneven and heels of any kind are not recommended.

Useful addresses

Telephone office In Livadi there is a small wooden sign in English
nailed to a tree on the left hand side of the *paralia* away from the
jetty but not visible on the walk towards the jetty. The office is
in the room of a house that belongs to a little old lady. The author
had great difficulty in making an international call from Serifos
and at times the meter started clicking over even though there was
no connection. The meter is across the room from the telephone
which makes monitoring the cost of the call difficult but if you

can understand what she says in Greek, the old lady will tell you when you reach the desired number of units. Try writing 100, 150 or whatever you require.

Stamps It is not possible to buy stamps in Livadi although sooner or later one of the shopkeepers will catch on to the 10% they are allowed to charge. (See under Hora.)

Money matters There is no bank on the island but the hotels will change travellers cheques and Eurocheques. For large amounts they may require notice of the transaction. It is best to change as much as you can at your port of arrival on the mainland.

Health There is no pharmacy on Serifos and apart from aspirins and liniment, the local shops do not stock anything you might need. (See under Hora.)

Centres of population

Livadi

This village is where the ferries now dock but in previous years the main port was at Mega Livadi, now disused. Livadi rambles around a cove at the bottom of the hillside of the town's capital, Hora. Edged with fine sand, backed with trees and dotted with moored, brightly painted kaiques, Livadi has a charming and peaceful atmosphere. The only concessions to tourists are a few hotels and two souvenir shops which still manage to blend with the surroundings. Most commercial buildings are along the the lined *paralia* with the jetty and harbour at one end. The main roads are the *paralia* (waterfront road) and a parallel road which is joined by a side street between the minimarket and bakery.

Hora

The island's capital sits on top of the hill above Livadi and its mostly white buildings give the effect of a snow capped hillside. The narrow stone flagged streets meander up and down between the houses and few shops. From the higher points of the town can be seen the old Kastro ruins with the stairway leading up to it.

Most activity is around the square, which is anything but square geometrically. Here are the four tavernas, a *cafenión* and the bus stop. If you want to rent a room in Hora, ask at the *cafenión*.

On the road from Livadi as it nears Hora, are most of the useful addresses. One hundred metres from Hora on the bend nearest the multicoloured church (red, blue, white and beige!) is the post office, easily identified by its bright yellow sign. No English is

Serifos. Hora. The island's capital appears to have melted down the sides of a peak like vanilla sauce on a Christmas pudding.

Serifos. This little church with its odd assortment of curves and angles is situated at the entrance to the islands port.

spoken so address your cards before buying stamps as you can present them to indicate what you need. Open from 07.30 to 14.30 hours Monday to Friday.

Further up from the post office, where the buildings commence at the left hand side of the road, is the police station, down some steps from the roadway. Look for the plaque above the doorway. The one policeman speaks a little English.

Five metres on further uphill on the same side of the road is the doctor's surgery. It is possible to buy medicines from the doctor without going through an examination, as long as you know what you need. When he is not in this little building there will be a phone number displayed on the door.

As the road finally reaches Hora, it forks. The right hand branch goes into the square while the left hand fork goes up past the telephone office which is located on the right hand side immediately after the fork. Open from 07.30 to 15.00 hours, seven days per week.

The next building up on the same side is a hardware store where the locals buy their petrol. On the other side of the road are the public lavatories.

Beaches

The beach at Livadi is the most attractive on the island and with its choice of shade under the trees or open golden sand, the only reason for moving elsewhere would be to look for a more secluded spot. The pathway leading up from the harbour by the side of the café passes a small church, with a roof of both angles and curves that give an unusual and charming effect, before going down the other side of the hill to a moderately sized sandy beach called Livadaki. In the opposite direction are the beaches of Ormos Leias, Ormos Ag. Sosti and Ormos Psili Amoss. On fine days small kaiques leave Livadi to take people to these more isolated beaches. (See "What to do".)

Historical background

Serifos has little in its history to differentiate it from the other Cyclades islands except for its iron and copper deposits that were mined at Mega Livadi until larger and more economical sources were discovered on the Greek mainland and in Africa. However,

Serifos. Livadi. This tiny and comparatively undeveloped bay is the main target for visitors. Centre picture on the crest of the hill is the island's capital reached by a long winding road that tests the suspension of vehicles making the journey.

the island's mythological significance is greater, as it was to the shores of Serifos that Princess Danae and her young son Perseus came after being cast adrift in a box by the King, Danae's father. The King was anxious to prevent the fulfilment of a prophecy that foretold his death at the hands of his grandson. He had previously locked his daughter in a tower but there she was visited by Zeus who fathered Perseus.

They were received on Serifos by King Polydectes who instantly took a liking to the beautiful princess and began to pursue her. His affections were not reciprocated and so he planned to be rid of Perseus who prevented him using more force in his wooing. After years of feigning disinterest, the King asked a favour of Perseus who was in his debt for the hospitality shown to him and his mother. The favour turned out to be a request for the head of Medusa, the Gorgon. The difficulty in acquiring this piece of anatomy came from the fact that the Medusa was so ugly with her hair of snakes, fang teeth and bulging eyes, that the mere sight of her turned humans to stone. Eternity as a statue might have been his fate had not the goddess Athena helped him by giving him a mirror-like shield, winged shoes and a cloak of invisibility.

While Perseus was thus occupied, his mother on Serifos was at the mercy of the King who tried to force her to marry him. On his return, Perseus found her taking refuge in the home of a fisherman who had been the first to find them when they were washed ashore years before. When he heard her story, the furious Perseus presented the surprised King and his banquet guests with Medusa's head and so all were turned to stone.

Having made the fisherman king, Perseus and Danae returned to the mainland. Danae's father fled but the prophecy was fulfilled in another town where Perseus killed him accidentally.

Serifos. Livadi. A caique is "dry-docked" for redecorating.

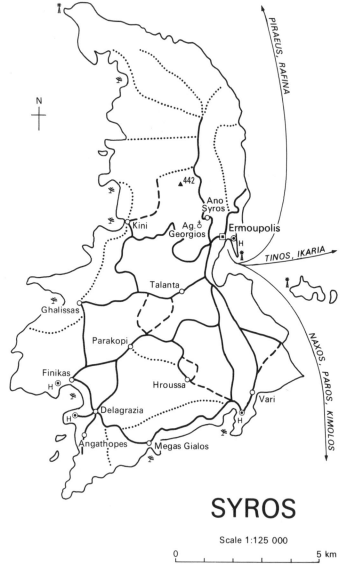

PIRAEUS, RAFINA

▲442

Ano
Syros

Ag.
Georgios

Kini

Ermoupolis
H

TINOS, IKARIA

Talanta

Ghalissas

Parakopi

NAXOS, PAROS, KIMOLOS

Finikas
H

Hroussa

Vari
H

Delagrazia
H

Angathopes

Megas Gialos

SYROS

Scale 1:125 000

0   5 km

For legend see inside front cover

FIFTEEN

Syros

Population 19,000   Highest point: 442 metres
Area: 87 sq. km.   Hotel beds: 1,700

As the ferry nears Ermoupolis, the main town of Syros, the houses can be seen to cover three hills, each with a conspicuously grand church near the summit. The houses along the waterfront are neoclassical and their somewhat dilapidated condition seems to enhance their charm.

To those who have visited other Cyclades islands, the variety of colour here is immediately noticeable in contrast to those islands where regulations permit the use of only white paint for the exterior walls. Untypically, great attention is paid to interior decor as well, with elaborate ceilings in houses and coffee bars, old and new.

Less picturesque but equally unique are the enormous dry docks and cranes that testify to Syros's shipbuilding industry.

At one time Syros was a much larger port than Piraeus, as it was the first safe port en route to the East prior to the construction of the Korinth Canal, and remained neutral during the war of independence under French protection.

During this time, many refugees from Chios, Psara and Smyrna flocked to Syros where they formed a settlement on the hillside now known as Vrontado. The refugees were largely Greek Orthodox, unlike the Catholic inhabitants, and so two separate communities and mayors existed.

During its more prosperous years, ship owners and captains built mansions in the vicinity of the orthodox church of St Nicholas in an area known as St Nicholas Place. This remains the influential residential area although some buildings are now given over to hotels, guest houses and government buildings.

The people of Syros went in search of the architect of La Scala in Milan and commissioned him to design for them a scaled down

Syros. A ferry arrives at the port viewed from the roof of the Cappucine monastery.

Syros. The town of Ermoupolis rises from the Venetian houses that line the waterfront up to the church and cathedral that crown the two hills.

replica. Celebrated artists and musicians performed at the theatre on tour from Milan until 1914. Today it is undergoing renovation but as there is some conflict about how this should be done, it may be some time before the work is completed.

Syros is the capital of the Cyclades and houses the judiciary, hospital, vehicle licensing and other government offices that serve all the islands in this group. While less prosperous now than in its heyday, Syros is still much visited by Greeks from neighbouring islands — where you will often be told, "You can't get it here, you have to go to Syros". Hence the island is used to visitors; but tourism is relatively new and it has given local businessmen the opportunity to organise its development.

Two categories of tourist visit the island: young travellers (often low budget) and family groups. As these two groups have different holiday requirements, they are subtly steered to separate locations.

Syros is not tourist-orientated like many of the more commercialised islands in the group and, although every effort is made to help and accommodate visitors, the priority is to maintain the present way of life. With a capacity of 1,700 beds and only 80 families involved in the tourist industry to date, they seem to be achieving that goal. Life goes on, with or without the foreigners, thus providing a chance to see an unadapted island even if not typical. For the same reason Syros is as active in winter as in the high season.

Arrival by sea

Syros is a major terminus for boats from both Piraeus and Rafina and for some travellers this may be the only reason for a visit here.

Ferry routes from Syros include:
- Paros, Naxos, Ios and Santorini
- Tinos, Mykonos
- Ikeria, Samos
- Paros, Amorgos, Astypalea, Kalymos, Kos, Nissyros, Tilos, Symi, Rhodes, Halki, Karpathos, Kassos and Crete
- Paros, Folegandros, Sikinos, Ios, Thirassia, Santorini and Anafi

The journey time from Piraeus to Syros is approximately four and a half hours. There is at least one sailing every day in winter for the mainland increasing in summer to upwards of four per day. Tickets for departure can be purchased at the numerous tourist offices along the waterfront, or on the boat from the purser's office. Boats do get full in summer and priority is given to ticket holders (although having purchased a ticket by no means guarantees your embarkation). You must have a valid ticket for a vehicle before you can drive on.

Road system

Except for the most northerly part of the island where even the dirt tracks become difficult to trace, the roads are of a high standard. In Ermoupolis, the network is largely a one-way system which is not always immediately obvious. The signposts are such that you can only read them if you are already going the wrong way! They show red circle and diagonal on blue background with white arrows pointing right and down.

Note that the road is one way towards the port police buildings (conspicuous by their arched frontage) or your first offence may be immediately on arrival! There is a wonderfully energetic policeman who supervises the loading and unloading of each ferry with almost non-stop whistle blowing. If you choose a waterfront setting for lunch, it provides interesting if noisy entertainment!

The main streets in town are paved with convex stones which make for a very bumpy ride. Out of town the two hills are ascended at as steep a gradient as is possible, giving rise to endless completely blind hairpin bends on which can be found parked cars at precisely the most dangerous places.

Maps can be bought at any of the book or souvenir shops and tourist offices. The most popular one is dotted with pictures of cars, buses and flowers to fill in the gaps between villages. Directions are in English as well as Greek and clearly mark the boundaries of each town or village.

Buses Buses leave from the waterfront in Ermoupolis and their destinations are clearly marked. They all take a circular route and timetables are found on the many town notice boards, in all tourist offices and most hotel and room receptions. There is no enquiry office. All routes are well served.

Taxis Syros has a large number of taxis which queue on two sides of the main square. Journeys to the top of either hill will not exceed the minimum charge of 75 drs. A journey to the discotheque at Ghalissas and back costs 750 drs. as the fare doubles after midnight. Take the first taxi in the queue. They work up until 03.00 or as long as there is a demand, and are familiar with all the eating places mentioned in this chapter.

Petrol There are numerous petrol stations in Ermoupolis but none

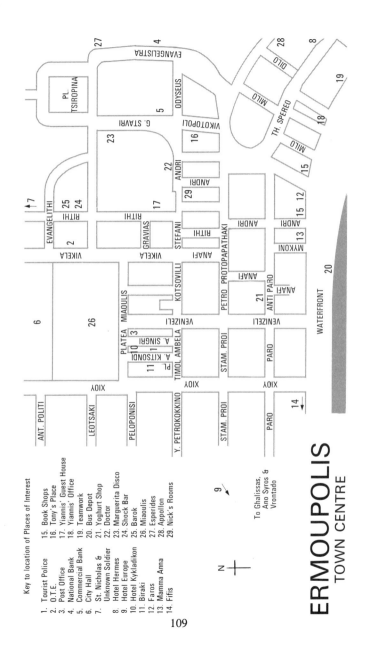

Key to location of Places of Interest

1. Tourist Police
2. O.T.E.
3. Post Office
4. National Bank
5. Commercial Bank
6. City Hall
7. St. Nicholas &
   Unknown Soldier
8. Hotel Hermes
9. Hotel Europe
10. Hotel Kykladikon
11. Biraki
12. Faros
13. Mamma Anna
14. Fifis
15. Book Shops
16. Tony's Place
17. Yiannis' Guest House
18. Yiannis' Office
19. Teamwork
20. Bus Depot
21. Yoghurt Shop
22. Doctor
23. Marguerita Disco
24. Shock Bar
25. Barok
26. Miaoulis
27. Esperides
28. Appollon
29. Nick's Rooms

To Ghalissas,
Ano Syros &
Vrontado

N

ERMOUPOLIS
TOWN CENTRE

109

outside the capital.

Ermoupolis, the capital

The main town and port has its commercial centre between the waterfront and Miaoulis Square in front of the town hall. The streets are mostly on a grid system with the odd curve thrown in on the exterior roads. Venizeli and Stam. Proi form a crossroads mid-way between the square and waterfront roads and Stam. Proi curves uphill to form the main route to the two hills of the town and other centres of population. All directions for Ermoupolis are given facing away from the sea on the waterfront with port police to the right and shipyards to the left.

The hill to your left is Ano Syros, the oldest part of the town and the setting for the Catholic Cathedral of St George and the Capuccine monastery. To the right, the hill Vrontado is crowned by the Orthodox church of Anastasis. Both hills are accessible either by road or endless steps. I recommend taking a 75 drs. taxi ride up and walking down as on the descent you can see your goal whereas on the ascent it is rather difficult to make out exactly where you are going apart from up!

Accommodation in Ermoupolis

There is accommodation available outside Ermoupolis and this is listed in the Centres of population section under the appropriate town.

Hotels
Accommodation like most things in Syros is expensive and what would be a D class hotel on Paros is a C or even B class here, both in price and standard.
— Hotel Hermes (B), tel: 28011. This conspicuous large white building to the left of the port police on the waterfront, has a stylish reception area and lounge. The style is less evident in the passageways and rooms but they are comfortable and clean. The hotel has been redecorating and developing but this did not cause any inconvenience to its guests.
— Hotel Europe (C), tel: 28771. Situated midway between the town centre and the roundabout where the exit roads meet, about five minutes walk from the square, this hotel was formerly the first

hospital in Syros. The rooms lead off from a charming courtyard where breakfast is served in summer.
— Hotel Cycladikon (D), tel: 22280. A "reception at the top of the stairs" style hotel facing the city hall; the rooms are clean but the staff somewhat unhelpful and a rather mausoleumlike atmosphere pervades. Communal bathrooms have a genuine but very uninviting bath.
— Hotel Aktaeon (E), tel: 22675. Clean comfortable rooms, communal bathroom. Concealed in O. Milos between the tourist offices along the waterfront.

Rooms
— Yiannis Guest House, tel: 28665. This guest house is very popular and Yiannis is proud of his courtyard where musician friends of his regularly gather to treat the guests to an atmospheric evening. He describes himself as "a clean freak" and nothing seems to belie this. The toilets and showers are on the ground floor, with the bedrooms and lounge on the first floor connected by an outside stairway. Yiannis plans to produce a street map and information handout for tourists as he believes there is a shortage of accurate information sources on the island. He also has about 5,000 books for sale or exchange. Follow the fluorescent orange signs that abound in the town.
— Tony's Place, no telephone. Guests have the use of kitchen facilities here. Some rooms are dormitory style and all use a communal bathroom. See map for location.
— Appollon Rooms, tel: 22158. These have a campus-like atmosphere with cosy lounge and good kitchen facilities, communal bathroom. Conspicuous yellow signposts begin around the tourist offices nearest the port police. These rooms are located in O. Odyseus.

Apartments
Most apartments for rent are located outside Ermoupolis. However, the best way of getting details is to enquire at the places displaying houses or apartments to rent signs, whether in an information office or in a private building.

Teamwork information office has details of apartments in all of the villages outside Ermoupolis but these often get full in summer.

Camping
No camping facilities exist in Ermoupolis and this is by design not

Syros. Ermoupolis. This waterside taverna is one of the many that provide an excellent place to watch the ferries come and go while you enjoy a leisurely lunch.

neglect. If you pitch a tent or attempt to sleep on a beach you will be moved on to Ghalissas.

Food

Folia Near the top of Ano Syros, Yiorgos has a large selection of unusual dishes including rabbit and pigeon. While perhaps slightly more expensive than its rivals, it is definitely worth a visit. Tables outside in summer. Excellent service. Recommended is the rabbit with baby onions.

Tembelis Further up the same hill, the name of this *taverna* means "lazy man" and the service can be a little slow in summer when locals have been known to fetch their own wine (from the barrel). The food is very good if a little on the oily side and is remarkable when you note that the kitchen is smaller than most toilets and the little old lady in black only has two hot plates on which to prepare all the food. Inside is the inevitable television together with a juke box (Greek music) that looks as if it came out of the ark! Tables outside in summer but the limited space is bordered by steep steps so be sure you can handle the retsina. Recommended is the fish with garlic sauce. Incredibly cheap.

Biraki Located in the smaller square just down and to the left of Miaoulis, this taverna serves only barbecued meat, fish and homemade hamburgers which are all tasty and tender. Service is efficient and courteous. Recommended are the *souvlaki* and *tsatsiki.*

Mama Anna On the right hand side of the waterfront, this restaurant is a good place to eat lunch and watch the boats come in. The chipped potatoes taste exactly like those from our own fish and chip shops.

Faros On the far right of the waterfront, this restaurant is popular with the locals. My meal was tasty but the meat was tough. It could have been an "off day". A few tables outside all year round.

Esperides (See map for location.) This converted mansion was described to the author as a private house unspoilt in its conversion. This it certainly is not but it provides a pleasant venue for up to 260 people to have a wide variety of coffees, cocktails and ice cream with or without pizza or spaghetti.

Barok This café/bar has a remarkable hallway more befitting a theatre than a café. Be sure to look up as you go up stairs as the ceiling is very ornate. Subdued blue/green lighting gives a romantic atmosphere enhanced by the live Greek music.

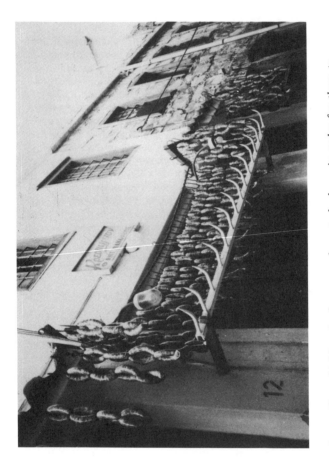

Syros. These highly spiced sausages have to be hung in order for them to mellow enough to make them palatable after which they are delicious.

114

Shock Bar Just five metres further down the hill from Barok, this bar has an equally notable ceiling although a century or two more recent in design. Loud disco music, comfortable chairs, steaks available. The shock is the price of the drinks!

Fifis Bar On the left of the waterfront this has very aromatic cognac and friendly service from Fifi and his Danish wife.

A small shop on O. Antiparo called Melissa sells home made yoghurt. In the main square there are numerous *ouzerias* and *cafenións,* some of which serve fish *mezes.* There is a large cake shop on the left hand corner of the waterfront and Venizeli that has a coffee shop annexe. I had a rather strange experience here while attempting to buy some cakes. Having pointed to what I wanted, the assistant asked me if I wanted to eat it on the premises. I looked around the shop that didn't have a single table or chair in sight and asked where exactly. He told me they had a *cafénion* next door and proceeded to unlock the adjoining door. When I got into the *cafenión* the selection was very poor in comparison to that in the shop and so I decided to revert to my original plan and take it back to my room. When I tried to go back through the adjoining door, it was locked so I went out onto the pavement and when I tried the door of the main shop, it too was locked! I went off very confused and cakeless!

The *cafenión* to the right at the bottom of the city hall steps seems to be rather clique and is very expensive.

Nightlife

Disco Marguarita Signposted from the right of the main square, this disco has quite reasonable decor and fairly up-to-date music. There is no entrance charge but a beer is 150 drs. The D.J. is very skilful at incorporating sound effects into each record though this does not always make it enjoyable to dance to.

Bazouki Lillis and Rahanos, both in Ano Syros, Nerida on the road to Vari, and Vrakos near Kini, are all open nightly in summer. Syros is the home of *bazouki* and proud of it. They have resisted changes in style apparent (but perhaps not to the uninitiated) in *bazoukis* on other islands.

Cinema Cine Pallas is open air in summer. This cinema changes its two film programme every three days. Showings are two hourly and begin at 4 p.m. The seats are very uncomfortable and the soft drinks warm. Up and right from city hall.

Concerts Concerts are held on Sundays by visiting local musicians.

Venue is either the old theatre or the club on the right hand corner of the city hall block. Look out for the posters: the word concert and the date are easily decipherable, the rest you can enquire about at the tourist offices.

A favourite and traditional weekend nocturnal pastime with the locals is the *Volta*. This is where family groups, usually with an eligible girl or boy, parade in their Sunday best up and down the main square. At first glance it is difficult to believe that they really do go back and forth continuously but watch someone who is conspicuously dressed, sure enough there they go again. This is the time to see and be seen and is the first step on the ladder to holy wedlock!

There are numerous video game and pool halls around Petro Protopapathaki (the right hand branch of the main horizontal road). The pool tables lack any markings on the baize and the holes seem larger — unless I am just underestimating my skill!

Useful addresses

Banks The Commercial Bank is just a bit farther down the hill from Disco Marguarita in G. Stavri Street and the National Bank is on the uphill fork from the end of Petro Protopapathaki where it becomes Evangelistra. Both are open from 08.00 to 13.30 Monday to Friday, with variable hours and days to supply the demand of visitors.

Doctor The turnover is fairly frequent but try behind the bronze plaques in Stefani. Tel. 24400 shop hours. In an emergency, the hospital is the large white building facing the roundabout on Stam. Proi. They are used to tourist casualties since helicopters ferry in unfortunates from the other islands, and there is always someone who speaks English.

Laundry There are no coin operated laundries in Syros but three deposit and collect laundries can be found in Petros Protopapathaki. The service is next day collection but this is not always reliable so try not to leave any cleaning until the last minute.

Post Office Large building with small doorway on the left hand corner of Venizeli and the main square. Open for stamps from 07.30 to 14.00 and for overseas parcels from 07.30 to 14.30, Monday to Saturday. Some English spoken.

Reading matter There are two bookshops next door but one to each other on the right of the waterfront, that sell English language books and newspapers year round. The average is a two-day delay, that is Monday's paper on Wednesday. A large selection for all tastes is available.

Telephone office On the right hand side, adjacent to city hall, the O.T.E. has six booths. These are unusual in having seats but not all have light bulbs. It is not possible to receive calls here but transfer charge or collect calls can be arranged by the English-speaking staff. Open 07.30 to 12 midnight.

Tourist information The staff in Teamwork (more conspicuous by its official looking blue 'Tourist Information' sign) speak English and are well clued up on what is available in the way of tours, hotel rooms, apartments, boat details as well as international bookings. Maps are on sale. Right hand side of the *paralia.*

Yiannis from the guest house has an information office with his orange sign outside on the right hand side of the waterfront. He is planning to produce an information sheet and street map. (The latter exists but is for the eyes of the military only and the author got some very suspicious looks while wandering around copying street names and trying to sketch roads.)

Tourist police This office is difficult to find, tucked away down the second side street to the left of where Venizeli meets the main square. Marked by an indistinct blue sign, it is the only doorway on that block. All the offices are up the stairs. They aim to have someone who speaks English every summer but were completely nonplussed when I asked for the address of an English-speaking doctor to recommend to you. Tel: 22620 or 22866.

What to see and do

The Unknown Soldier The first ever memorial to an Unknown Soldier is in Ermoupolis in front of St Nicholas church in a pleasant garden. Unfortunately the small gates are kept locked so it is difficult to get a good photograph.

Church of St Nicholas (the patron saint of seamen) is well worth a visit. It has a famous painting of the Last Supper and a painting by El Greco was recently discovered inside. The latter is now being restored in Athens before being returned to the church. The best time to visit the church is in the morning and entrance is not via the main doors at the top of the steps but round to the right where the multilingual signs request the respect due to a holy place.

Capuchin Monastery This is the home of Father Dimitrios Freres who speaks French, German and Italian but not English. He has lived alone there for 35 years and is an excellent host who is eager

Syros. The yearly service at the memorial to The Unknown Soldier that was the first of its kind anywhere in the world.

to impart the history of both the monastery and Syros. He speaks slowly for foreigners (by no means common among Greeks) and welcomes visitors. The best way to contact him is via the Teamwork tourist office (see Useful addresses) as he calls there most mornings between 11.00 and 12 noon after making his rounds of various villages. It would take four pages of description to describe to you how to find the monastery on foot starting at the point where the taxi would drop you. So either say "Monastéerio" and look puzzled at anyone you meet or wait for the Father at the tourist office.

En route, be sure to note where the angles of the houses have been rounded off to aid the passage of the donkeys and mules that brought supplies to the monks. The monastery buildings are not remarkable but Father Dimitrios has some sixteenth century books and manuscripts and the church is a grand viewpoint for Ermoupolis. A suitable gift in repayment for his courtesy is a packet of filter cigarettes (forgive me Father, I can't remember the brand!). Tel. 22576. On the way down note the Orthodox cemetery with its grand mausoleums and monuments and memorials. Further up the hill is the Catholic cathedral of St George.

Loukoumi The Greeks consider that the best *loukoumi* (known to us as Turkish Delight) is made in Syros and numerous shops selling only this and local soft nougat are found on the waterfront. It is possible to see it being made in the vicinity of these shops. Enquire at Teamwork (see Useful addresses). No charge is made but you will be expected to buy some of the product.

Orphanage and handicrafts On the road to Kini is an unsignposted side road near the red roofed monastery of Ag. Barbara. The monastery is the home of 17 female orphans who produce handicrafts, including rugs and woven fabrics, which are for sale in the little shop.

Church of the Anastasis On the very top of the hill community Vrontado, this is another place deserving of a taxi ride up — 75 drachma. This is the main Orthodox church on the island and has a remarkable painting on the inside of the huge domed ceiling. Should it be closed, enquire at the priest's house on the immediate left of the church.

The Museum Up the steps to the left of the city hall from the square is a museum that is well worth a visit (though the author cannot verify this as on each attempt to visit it was closed — the explanation given was that the caretaker's superior is based on Mykonos!) Theoretical opening hours 09.00 to 15.00 Monday to Saturday, 10.00 to 14.00 Sunday. Closed on Tuesday. Free admission.

Syros. This tower is the gateway to the cemetery where many elaborate mausoleums and shrines have been built.

Xalandrianis and Kastri There are archaeological sites here, both very difficult to find without a guide such as a taxi driver, and at least 20 minutes walking is involved. These sites are not of major significance in the world of archaeology and apparently are seldom visited.

Tours and excursions From May to October, Teamwork Tourist Information Office run three tours using 14-seater buses.

- The first takes approximately four hours and visits all the villages and beaches on the southern half of the island. Cost 1,100 drachmas.
- The second tour is of the town of Ermoupolis including Ano Syros and Vrontido. Cost 1,400 drachmas inclusive of lunch.
- The third is Syros by night. It costs 1,400 drachmas including dinner.

Yiannis information office can arrange round the island boat trips if there are sufficient numbers of people.

Motorbikes and mopeds can be hired from many offices near the waterfront and they advertise this facility.

Beaches

Individual beaches are described in detail under the appropriate town. Those of most note are Kini, Gallisas, Vari, Megas Gialos and Finikas.

There are numerous secluded sandy beaches to the north of the island but after Kiperoussa the road becomes a dirt track and eventually disappears altogether. In other words, the local attitude is that if you want a really secluded beach, you are going to have to look hard for it, which guarantees them remaining secluded! This seems fair enough and therefore no secret locations are going to be revealed here!

Nude sunbathing and swimming are unofficially tolerated at San Bakou, a ten minute walk south of the main beach at Ghalissas.

Centres of population

Vari
While the village of Vari is nothing to look at, it has a good sandy beach that offers safe swimming. Hotels in Vari are:
— Ahladi (C), tel: 61400; 25 beds.
— Domenica (C), tel: 61216; 37 beds.

Ano Syros. One of the winding streets that lead up to the Cappucine monastery. The corners of the houses have been rounded off to enable the donkeys to carry wider loads.

— Kamelo (C), tel: 61217; 45 beds.
— Emily (D), tel: 61213; 14 beds.

Restaurant Volas has a large selection of fish on the menu and the neighbouring café has rooms to rent.

Megas Gialos

At right angles to a hillside covered with incedibly brightly painted houses, is a long thin sandy beach backed with trees and paddle boats. Hotels in Megas Gialos are:
— Akrotiri (C), tel: 42142; 41 beds.
— Alexanda (C), tel: 42540; 58 beds.

The waterfront *cafenion* has a prize collection of plastic geraniums in pots and the interior designer must have been anxious to break with tradition as many of these are positioned on the walls almost upside down. One of the window boxes holding real geraniums has been carefully painted with the words "I love u you hear?"!

Finikas

Finikas, or Phoenix, has a long thin sandy beach rather exposed to the road. Hotels in Finikas are:
— Finikas (C), tel: 42111; 25 beds.
— Olympia (C), tel: 42212; 78 beds.
— Cyclades (E), tel: 42255; 23 beds.

Hotel Finikas on the hillside serves coffee and pizza. There are also cafés Theresa and Cyclades.

Possidonia

This is a pretty little village with a harbour for small boats. Just outside the village towards Finikas is a church that has been painted entirely blue. Only one of the three doors had a handle and this was locked so the author could not view the interior. The beach is sandy but there are some stones beneath the waterline. The Greek flag marks the site of a small naval base. There is a café called Delagrazia; hotels in Possidonia are:
— Delagrazia (B), tel: 42225; 19 beds.
— Eleana (C), tel: 42601; 51 beds.
— Poseidonion (C), tel: 42300; 109 beds.

Kini

Kini is larger than the other villages and has two long sandy beaches, an *ouzeria,* shop, disco, bar and two restaurants. However, there are no hotels here.

Syros. The hills of Ano Syros and Vrontado with the church of the Anastasis crowning the hill to the right.

Syros. The church of the anastasis on the hill of Vrontado. The island of Didimi and its lighthouse guard the entrance to the harbour.

Ghalissas

There are hardly enough houses here to call it a village but in summer it hosts the more active of the island's visitors. There is a long stretch of sandy beach that gets pretty crowded in season and ten minutes walk to the south over a small rise of land is a more secluded beach that tolerates nudism.

There are two bars, two discos and three hotels at Ghalissas:
— Francoise (C), tel: 42000; 48 beds.
— Romantica (C), tel: 61211; 58 beds.
— O. Petros (E), no telephone; 18 beds.

Camping Giana is the only camp site on the island at present and its facilities include a shop, equipment hire and full washing and toilet facilities.

Wind surfing and water skiing are found here. Details from the camp ground which is fully signposted until you get to a T-junction with a choice of left or right and no clues. Take the left, this also leads to the beach. This is the only place on the island where cattle sheds are evident, giving a very rural setting for what becomes a hotbed of activity.

Historical background

Syros's first inhabitants were the Phoenicians who made settlements at Dellagracia and Finikas. The island is proud to be the home of the philosopher Ferekides who was the teacher of Pythagaros and designer of the Heliotropion, the first observatory in history which was founded here and was connected in some way with the worship of Poseidon.

The population moved to the hill of Ano Syros in Ermoupolis in the thirteenth century to escape raiding pirates. In the same century the Venetians converted all but eight families of the islanders to Catholicism and when the Turks invaded in 1566 religious tolerance was observed.

During the War of Independence in 1822, Syros was protected by France and it was to this island that refugees from Psara Chios and Smyra fled. The refugees founded an Orthodox settlement on the neighbouring hill of Vrontado and so two separate communities existed as they still do today.

The majority of the island's population live in the capital and there are very few settlements elsewhere on the island.

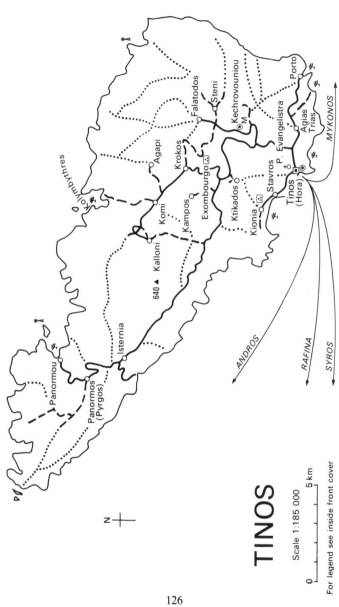

TINOS

Scale 1:185 000

For legend see inside front cover

0   5 km

N

Panormou
Panormos (Pyrgos)
Isternia
Kolymbythres
640 ▲ Kalloni
Kampos
Komi
Agapi
Krokos
Exombourgo
Falatodos
Steni
Kechrovouniou
M
Ktikados
Kionia
Stavros
Tinos (Hora)
P. Evangelistra
Agias Trias
Porto
MYKONOS
ANDROS
RAFINA
SYROS

SIXTEEN

Tinos

Population: 9,000   Highest point: 640 metres
Area: 195 sq. km.   Hotel beds: 1,428

Tinos is an island of hills and valleys in which nestle its 64 villages. Like many other islands, the population has decreased in recent years leaving some of the villages almost deserted.

The island has 890 white painted and ornately carved Venetian pigeon houses. The birds are now kept as pets and as a food source and in former years the droppings were used to fertilise the soil.

The hillsides have been fashioned into terraces, maintained by old stone walls. Although the soil is fertile, no crops are grown on the land and sheep and goats graze unhindered.

The main town, also called Tinos, is on the south-east coast of this pear-shaped island. Few of the other villages receive visitors with the exception of Pyrgos and Kekrovouni; however a bus or hire car journey is well worthwhile to see these little clusters of white houses with their many and varied churches in sharp contrast to the hillside background.

In Tinos town at the top of the hill that rises gently from the port, is the splendid walled church of Panayia Evangelistra, often referred to as the "Greek Lourdes". It is to this church that pilgrims go in their tens of thousands on 25 March and 15 August. Hence Tinos is used to visitors but the non-Greek tourist industry is comparatively new. Evidence of its existence is plain as you approach the port on arrival, as there is an enormous hotel just to the north of the harbour which is used by two of Britain's largest tour operators.

The port of Tinos seen from the ferry where many of the day trip vessels await the start of the season.

The island is by no means a swinging centre of night life but there are adequate facilities for those who want them.

The island has many beaches which are all long narrow strips of sand where it is possible to swim safely and comfortably. On the rocky shoreline you can see evidence of the green marble found on Tinos.

Arrival by sea

There are daily services to both Piraeus (via Syros) and Rafina (via Andros). Tinos also has daily connections to Paros, Naxos and Mykonos with a twice weekly service to the Dodecanese, Rhodes and Crete.

Sailing details can be confirmed at the port police office next door to the pharmacy on the corner of O. Ierarhon and the *paralia,* second floor. Tickets are available at the numerous offices that display the names of the ferries in metre-high letters above the doors. You must have a ticket for any vehicle you plan to take on board.

The largest boats dock at the end of the concrete jetty while the smaller ones come in to the quayside. Ask when you buy your ticket where your boat leaves from, especially if you have a vehicle to position or heavy luggage to move.

Road system

The island's roads are mostly asphalted and in good condition. The unmade road from Ellenikaria to Komi deteriorates rapidly after rain and bends must be negotiated with care in view of the sheer drop from the side of the road. However, this is a short cut and not an essential route.

Maps can be purchased at any of the souvenir shops and there are at least three to choose from. Toubi's is the easiest to follow while the one with a picture of a dovecot on the front entitled Tourist map of Tinos gives detail in symbols as to where various species of wildlife can be found. All maps give a concise history of the island together with suggestions of places of interest to visit.
Taxis Taxis queue at the corner of O. Ierarhon and the *paralia* and except on pilgrimage days and just after a boat docks, there are always some waiting for hire. One of the island's characters is Christos, a taxi driver who, as he will proudly inform you, has

Tinos. Christos the famous taxi-driver amusing two of the girls who weave carpets with amazingly intricate patterns at the Nunnery of Orsolinas

Tinos. The girls at the Nunnery of Orsolinas have such dexterity at their carpet weaving that in order to see how it is actually done, you have to ask them to slow down.

130

already been mentioned in at least two guide books. He will delight in taking you round the island pointing out places of interest and giving little snippets of information in Greek, English, French or Italian that he learns in his spare time.

Buses Buses (mid blue) leave from the waterfront and details of fares and schedules are available at the office opposite the departure point next to the National Bank.

Petrol There are garages on both roads leading out of Tinos town.

Tinos town: Hora

The hotels and ticket offices that face out to sea seem taller than those found on other islands. This is perhaps because of the spaces between them and variations in design. Any picturesque quality of the area comes from the gaily painted fishing boats moored in the harbour.

Facing Panayia Evangelistra, the waterfront road becomes a one way system as it heads out of town: right towards Porto and Triantaros, and left to Stavros and beyond.

At right angles to the *paralia* are three parallel roads. the two left ones lead up to the church while the third turns off to the right. Farthest left, O.L. Megaloharis was designed to cope with the great number of pilgrims that make their way uphill and so is very wide. The Post Office and O.T.E. are on the right of this road near the top. The museum is at the top on the left and in front of the church the road is cobbled and curves to join the middle road that is as narrow as the first is wide. Most of the shops are in this narrow street which, although it does get some traffic in winter, is pedestrian only in summer. Between the taxi rank and the pharmacy is the third road, O. Ierarhon. These three roads are connected by side streets of varying width and straightness that contain *tavernas* and shops among the houses.

Some of the buildings in town are owned by the monastery of Loutra, donated by women joining the order of nuns.

The shops display icons, medallions, incense and votive plaques. The latter are shaped to represent the part of the body suffering the affliction to be cured, such as eyes, legs, arms, etc. Candles hang by their wicks from the ceilings (some of them only just hang as they can be two metres long!) and pilgrims stagger uphill with these to offer in the church. There are also the more ordinary shops with a limited selection of souvenirs. If buying postcards, be sure to read the inscription on the back as for some reason, they also

131

sell a large number of views of Mykonos!

Accommodation

During the festivals on 25 March and 15 August, it is impossible to find a bed; however at other times you should have no problems. Mini buses from hotels and individuals with rooms to let meet the boats all year round.

Hotels There are at least 30 hotels in Tinos town but surprisingly few in the other villages.

— Alonia Hotel (B), tel: 23541-43. Although this hotel is 1.5 km from the town, it runs an hourly minibus service into town which leaves from outside the café on the far right of the waterfront and opposite the war memorial. Comfortably furnished, the hotel has a swimming pool and a disco, although the latter may be for residents only to prevent noise from vehicles departing in the early hours. It has facilities for overseas calls dialled direct from its rooms individually metered. Bar, snack bar, restaurant.

— Afrodite (C), tel: 22456. Take the far right hand road that passes in front of Hotel Oceanis and take the first left. This hotel is a white building on the opposite corner. It is family run and has a pleasant atmosphere with its local decor and friendly staff. Bar, snacks.

— Byzantion (C), tel: 22454. (Also written as Vyzantion). Another traditionally decorated hotel with clean, comfortable rooms. Bar, snack bar, TV lounge.

— Oceanis (C), tel: 22452. This large hotel is on the right of the harbour and you can't fail to notice it as your ferry approaches. Ground floor restaurant is open all day.

— Eleana (D), tel: 22561. To the right of the little church, one block past the police sign in O. Ierarhon about 200 m away, this clean friendly hotel gives great value for money and the rooms are of a better standard than those of many (C) class hotels.

— Aigli (D), tel: 22240. (Also written as Aegli). This one is on the left of the harbour above its restaurant. Some rooms have private bath, others have only basin. Key to shower room costs extra.

Tinos. With the benefit of colour, this would be a good example of how the local people contrive to introduce a splash of colour to the streets with flamboyant paintwork on windows and doors and by growing flowers in every available container.

Accommodation summary

	Category	Telephone	Beds
Tinos Beach (Kionia)	A	22626	339
Aeolos Bay	B	23339	131
Alonia	B	23541	64
Favie Souzane	B	22693	63
Theoxenia	B	22274	59
Tinion	B	22261	47
Afrodite	C	22456	22
Argo	C	22588	20
Asteria	C	22132	92
Avra	C	22242	31
Delfinia	C	22289	73
Flisvos	C	22243	66
Galini	C	22260	15
Golden Beach	C	22579	19
Leto	C	22791	36
Meltemi	C	22881	77
Oassis	C	23055	43
Oceanis	C	22452	91
Poseidon	C	23123	73
Rafaelo	C	23072	16
Vyzantion (or Byzantion)	C	22454	54
Aegli (or Aigli)	D	22240	24
Acroyali	D	-	24
Eleana	D	22561	24
Thalia	E	22811	25

Apartments and rooms There seems to be a shortage of apartments on Tinos and there are very few "rooms" signs. Try behind the blocks on the left of the harbour.
— Golden Beach Bungalows, tel: 22579 23168. These nicely furnished apartments have fridge, cooker and crockery provided in the kitchens. All rooms in the larger block have a view of the long sandy beach, which is just twenty metres away from the balcony. It is 1½ kilometres out of town; the owner Mr Nicolaos Souranis operates a mini bus service. Café, snack bar. Easy reach for the two out of town discos. The family apartments sleep five. Enquiries can be made at Tinos Mariner 300 metres north along the *paralia* — wave this book at them and they promise a 10% discount!

Camping Blue signs for the camp site start at the harbour and 150 metres away, the facilities include equipment rental, showers and a snack bar.

Boats The Tinos Mariner tourist office provides weather reports, showers, engine servicing, ice blocks and information for seafarers. It is near the second harbour 300 metres along the *paralia* to the left.

Food

The eating places seem to be of a similar standard throughout the town. Worth a try are:

Palia Palladia The nicest way to find it is to walk left along the *paralia* until you see a fountain with dolphins on your right behind which the blue and white sign is visible (30 metres). Thirty tables, wine from the barrel and a *bazouki* handy for anyone who feels like playing it. Recommended: roast pork.

Kypos Third turning on the left along O. Ierarhon, five metres down on the right. The name means "garden" but although the garden at the rear has been described in print as "lush" this must have been before they concreted it. Slightly surly service but an excellent herby Greek salad.

Fanaria This one is along the *paralia* about twenty metres past Palia Palladia; the *dolmades* are very good.

All the cafés are on the *paralia*. Out of Hora try Yiamas Taverna at Krokos and Miousis at Kalloni.

Night Life

At one time discotheques had to be built outside the town in deference to its religious standing. Today there are at least two bars in the centre of town that advertise nightly Greek dancing. **Discos** B.B's and Asterixs are both about fifteen minutes walk from the town along the *paralia* to the right. Tinos Beach Hotel Disco is not surprisingly situated at the Tinos Beach Hotel, 45 minutes walk along the *paralia* to the left. Taxis wait outside all of these discos in the summer.

Bars Georges Place 2 is along the left hand side of the *paralia* behind the dolphin fountain and next door to Palia Palladia. George speaks excellent English and has a nice line in chat! From surely the highest bar stools ever encountered you can watch the Greek dancing and disco, or climb off and join it! Zorbas Bar 30 metres past the fountain to the left of the *paralia,* is a compact bar, has Greek dancing and a wide selection of music.

Useful addresses

Police and emergencies The office on the left hand side of the second turning left along O. Ierarhon and well signposted; little English is spoken but they are very friendly. If you really need help with language — say in an emergency — consult Tinos Mariner (see next address). Tel: 22255.

Tinos Mariner The tourist office is near the second harbour along the *paralia* to the left. The owner, Andonis Foskolos, speaks five languages including English and is called upon to act as official interpreter when needed. He is always willing to help out and has details of any current English-speaking doctors on the island or will interpret for you. Tel: 23193 or 22707.

Postal and telephone office On the right hand side of O. Megaloharis near the top, both agencies are in one building. Stamps and overseas parcels 07.30 to 14.30 hours. Telephone services from 07.30 to 16.00 hours Monday to Saturday, closed Sundays. There are international call boxes along the *paralia*.

Banks The National Bank of Greese is along the *Paralia* between O. Ierarahon and the smaller unnamed street. The Commercial Bank of Greece is on the far left of the *paralia,* opposite the jetty. Hours from 08.00 to 14.30 hours Monday to Thursday and 08.00 to 14.00 hours Friday.

Reading matter Next to the Commercial Bank is a bookshop which

Tinos. Krokos. Two of the lunchtime regulars at the little taverna.

clearly advertises its stock of English newspapers and books, summer only.

What to see and do

This section also includes other centres of population as the villages have little or no accommodation facilities.

Nunnery of Kechrovouniou In June of 1822, Pelagia, a nun from the Kechrovounion Nunnery had a series of dreams in which the Virgin Mary revealed to her that an icon was buried on a nearby farm. After several months of digging, the ruins of a Byzantine church were found and eventually on 30 January 1823 the icon was unearthed by a workman. The church of Panayia Evangelistra was built on the site of the find and the icon is displayed inside.

The nunnery has 76 nuns, many of whom come from the mainland. Apart from taking meals alone, the life is not as hard as in Pelagia's day. Her cell is open to the public and some fairly recent paintings depict the vision that took place there.

A new church has been built within the grounds of the nunnery from the donations of pilgrims and its white marble is a sharp contrast to the usually dimly lit churches of Greece. Pelagia's skull is kept in a glass box within this church for visitors to kiss as a demonstration of faith and for luck.

Catholic Nunnery of Orsolinas Ten kilometres from Hora, there are hourly buses. While the architecture of the buildings is unremarkable, the nunnery has a weaving school for local girls from poor families to teach them a trade and provide some income. It is the home of a delightful Canadian nun who is now 90 years old and has lived in Greece for 35 years. She is always pleased to hear news of home. Until 1984, the nunnery also had an orphanage but this is now closed as there is no longer a demand.

Church of Panayia Evangelistra Built on the top of the hill in Hora where the icon was found in 1823, this large-walled complex houses many museums displaying icons from all over the world and the gifts of pilgrims — which include many fine paintings, ornate ivory and wood carvings and jewellery.

The main church is festooned with hundreds of incense burners presented to the church by its visitors. The miracle-working icon is rather difficult to see as it has been decorated with jewels, pearls and precious metals. Pilgrims kiss the glass case and pray for a cure for whatever ails them or for good fortune.

During the festivals, so many candles are offered with prayers that they have to be removed almost as soon as they are lit to cope with the demand for space.

Below the main church is a crypt where the children from all over Greece are brought to be baptised. On 15 August 1940, an Italian submarine torpedoed and sank the "Elle", a Greek cruise ship, while it was docked in the harbour having brought pilgrims to the festival. A mausoleum on the lower left of the complex has been built in memory of those killed.

Admission to the museums is 50 drachmas and 30 drachmas for students. Opening hours are 08.30 to 20.30 but this tends to be variable. The safest bet is just after a ferry boat arrives at the port or shortly after services.

Holy Trinity Church At Ag. Trios, two kilometres from Hora, is the small Holy Trinity church and cemetery maintained by a little old man who speaks no English. He will, however, be pleased to admit you to the rooms that were used as a clandestine school run by priests, during the time of the Turkish occupation, for children from neighbouring villages whose parents were anxious for them to receive a Greek education. Another room houses examples of the carved marble semi-circles that decorate the arches above the island's doorways.

Archaeological Museum A sandy coloured building at the top of O. Megaloharis, just down from the church, this museum has a reputation for erratic opening hours despite its claims to open 08.30 to 12.30 and 16.00 to 18.00 Monday to Saturday, 10.00 to 14.00 hours Sundays and closed all day Tuesdays. Entrance fee is 50 drachmas and 30 drachmas for students. The small collection includes finds from Exombourgo and Kioni.

Ruins Exombourgo was the site of the island's acropolis and the remains of walls and towers can be seen at the top of the hill where the 3,000 inhabitants lived. Their water supply was at the bottom of the hill and this remains in reasonable condition. Exombourgo has been little excavated but plans exist for this and for forty other sites. Kioni has the remains of the fourth-century temple of Poseidon and Amphitrite.

School of Art Tinos has produced many of Greece's renowned artists and sculptors and today the tradition continues at the School of Art in Pyrgos. Just outside Pyrgos, towards Platia, there is a family workshop where marble and wood are carved into figurines and chests. The work is for sale and the entrance is marked by large signs proclaiming traditional arts and tourist souvenirs.

Excursions Two separate round the island tours operate in summer. They call at many of the more interesting villages including

The islands port seen from the ferry with the grand church waiting at the top of the hill for it's pilgrims.

Tinos. The Church of Panayia Evangelistra in the main town is the destination for thousands of pilgrims every year and is known as the "Lourdes of the Aegean".

140

Kekrovouni, Loutra, Komi, Exombourgos, Falatados, Ktikados, Pyrgos and Panormos where there is time for lunch and a quick swim. 09.00 to 15.30 hours, 500 drachmas. Tickets available from any of the travel offices. Enquire as to whether this year's guide speaks English.

Five times per week the boat Megalohari leaves on a day trip to Mykonos and Delos. No guide is provided but at Delos there are guides for hire to show you around the wealth of archaeological remains.

Centres of population

The many villages of Tinos all have individual character and at least a day can be enjoyably spent touring the island either by taxi or hired car or motorbike.

Krokos
Krokos is an attractive little village with a café/bar called Yia mas. It also has a cross between a *taverna* and a shop, where Ioistina cooks delicious and unusual food while the little old ladies gather in a corner to chatter. Rooms for rent are available here, also from Yia mas.

Isternia
This is a large picturesque village that leaps out at you from around a bend in the road. It is between here and Pyrgos that the green marble is quarried. All the local families are involved in this prosperous industry and the houses are consequently large and opulent.

Agias Trias
Apart from the church of the Holy Trinity already described, this little village has another attractively decorated church of Ag. Barbara. Following the same road to the coast brings you to two of the island's best beaches at Porto.

Pyrgos
Pyrgos has an artistic tradition as it is the birthplace of many of Greece's most wellknown artists. Today the school of art and weaving school endeavour to continue this tradition. It is possible to eat and stay here or four kilometres further north on the coast at Panormos.

Tinos. Krokos. This small village is one of the 64 that are scattered about the islands hills and valleys. On the curve of the road is the taverna/shop/cafe that makes this village well worth a visit.

Panormos

This is a small harbour that just escapes being picturesque and not only because of what appears to be graffiti painted in large white letters on the harbour wall. It is in fact welcoming visitors but nevertheless spoils the appearance.

During the second world war, four ships were sunk at Ag. Petros and the German crews scurried up the hillside to the neighbouring villages. My guide was unable to tell me what became of them.

Port Stavros

This was the original port of Tinos and the ruins of the old jetty can still be seen. The little village of Karia with ten houses and 24 churches has only five families still living there. At Xinara the island's Catholic bishop lived in a very grand house that is now open to visitors.

Beaches

The nearest beach to Hora is Ag. Fokas, a very long narrow sandy beach twenty minutes walk away. Snacks are available from the café at Golden Beach bungalows.

On the other side of town, the *paralia* road leads out to Kioni where Tinos Beach Hotel complex backs on to the first of four sandy beaches separated by rocky projections that require sensible shoes to negotiate them. The farthest beach is sheltered even when the wind turns other beaches into sandstorms. Nudism is tolerated here but it is a better idea to explore the north coast of the island if you seek a secluded beach. Hourly buses go to the hotel from Hora.

Panormos beach is popular in summer. The buses go here from Hora twice daily and the little harbour has cafés and a *taverna*.

After a scenic bus ride to Komi, three kilometres further north on a good road is the beach of Kolymbythres. This beach is never crowded, probably because it is not served by public transport. Snacks are available and there are plans for a camping ground here.

Eight kilometres south east from Hora is the village of Porto where two glorious beaches offer safe swimming. Divided by a narrow strip of land, the second beach is the most inviting. Snacks are available and a camping ground is planned. At the moment, this village is not on the bus route but check at the office in town.

Historical background

Tinos has had a fairly eventful history and knows many different masters. The original inhabitants were Ionians from Karia who were invaded by the Persians in 490 B.C. and were under their occupation until they were liberated after the Battle of Marathon in 478 B.C. The island then came under Athenian rule until 338 B.C. when it was conquered by the Macedonians. In the meantime the war between Rome and Mithridates left Tinos in ruins. After defeat at the hands of the Romans, Rhodians and King Attalus of Pergamon, the island had been stripped of all its wealth.

Two towns existed on the island, both were named Tinos. One remains today, the capital or Hora, and the other was on higher and safer ground at Exombourgo where a fortress was built by the Venetians who invaded in 1390. The islanders were notorious pirates at this time. In 1570, the Turks unsuccessfully attacked the fortress incurring heavy losses. This was to happen on another ten occasions after which the Turks often destroyed the rest of the island's settlement. By 1715, the rest of Greece had succumbed to Turkish occupation but Tinos held firm until a massive fleet arrived once more to attack Exombourgo. The Venetians decided that they stood no chance of winning against such a force and surrendered to the amazed Turks who gave them safe conduct to Venice. A poignant end to this episode of history is that on their return to Venice they were executed for treason as it was assumed they must have been bribed to surrender.

Many of the 19,000 islanders fled to Africa and the Sultan presented Tinos to his Treasurer as a gift. Life continued under the supervision of three local dignitaries.

Tinos was active during the War of Independence in 1821 and in 1823 the famous holy icon was discovered. The Junta declared the whole island a holy place and regulations were enforced regarding behaviour and dress.

The mythology connected with Tinos tells that the god Aeolus lived in a cave on the island's highest mountain from where he caused gales to wreak havoc on the Cyclades islands. The god Poseidon took Tinos under his care and cast out the disproportionate number of snakes that lived there.

Various theories exist about how the island got its name. These include that the name derived from that of the first inhabitant and from the Phoenician word *tanoth* meaning snakes. It has also been known as Hydrousa, as the island has always had a plentiful supply of water which is a rarity among Greek islands.